William Smith, C.G.F Dumas

Historical Account of Bouquet's Expedition Against the Ohio

Indians, in 1764

William Smith, C.G.F Dumas

Historical Account of Bouquet's Expedition Against the Ohio Indians, in 1764

ISBN/EAN: 9783337328689

Printed in Europe, USA, Canada, Australia, Japan

Cover: Foto ©ninafisch / pixelio.de

More available books at **www.hansebooks.com**

HISTORICAL ACCOUNT

OF

Bouquet's Expedition

AGAINST THE OHIO INDIANS,

IN 1764.

WITH PREFACE BY FRANCIS PARKMAN,
Author of "Conspiracy of Pontiac," etc.

AND

A TRANSLATION OF DUMAS'
BIOGRAPHICAL SKETCH OF GENERAL BOUQUET.

CINCINNATI, O.
ROBERT CLARKE & CO.
1868.

The Indians giving a Talk to Colonel Bouquet in a Conference at a Council Fire, near his Camp on the Banks of Muskingum in North America, in Oct.r 1764.

PUBLISHERS' NOTICE.

IN offering to our patrons the *Account of General Bouquet's Expedition against the Ohio Indians in* 1764, as the first of the reprints of the OHIO VALLEY HISTORICAL SERIES, we may premise that we have been urged thereto by the rarity of the volume and its intrinsic value as an authentic and reliable narrative of one of the earliest British military expeditions into the *Territory North-West of the Ohio River*.

This work was published at Philadelphia in 1765, reprinted at London the following year; and an edition in French, by C. G. F. DUMAS, was issued at Amsterdam in 1769.

Mr. FRANCIS PARKMAN has kindly furnished us with a few prefatory words. The proper introduction, however,

however, to this work, and indeed to all the fragmentary accounts of the later struggles of the white and Indian races in the Central West, is his "History of the Conspiracy of Pontiac," of which this expedition was one of the results. We can not too earnestly recommend its perusal to our readers. His wonderfully clear and exact knowledge of Indian character, and its faithful portrayal in his introductory chapters, together with his minute accounts of their tribal divisions, their internal differences, their modes of warfare, the nature of their governments, and his general review of the "situation," can not fail to be of great service in attaining an intelligent understanding of the story of the Indian wars in the West, and the trials and hardships of the sturdy pioneers, whose bloody struggles and anxious labors laid the foundation of the present prosperity of this region.

Mr. PARKMAN has also translated for us M. DUMAS' biographical sketch of GENERAL BOUQUET prefixed to the French edition. We regret that we are, at present, unable to give a more detailed history of his transactions in this country, the most active and interesting period of his life, concerning which M. DUMAS' sketch is very meagre, passing over in silence his important services as one of the commanders of the *Royal American Corps*, his connection with the former expedition against *Fort Duquesne,*

Duquesne, in 1758, under GENERAL FORBES, and his celebrated controversy with General—then Colonel—WASHINGTON as to the route which that expedition should take from *Carlisle* to *Fort Duquesne*.* The one urgently advocated by GENERAL BOUQUET, through *Raystown*, now *Bedford*, and *Loyal Hanna*, was adopted, and the marked advantage of this road in subsequent military operations, and in encouraging the settlement of *Western Pennsylvania*, evinced his practical wisdom and forethought.

We would call the attention of our readers to the successful manner in which, by the " *Osborne Process*," the American Photo-Lithographic Company have reproduced the map, plans, and the two plates by BENJAMIN WEST, in *fac-simile* of the originals.

For facility of reference, an index has been added.

---

* For particulars of this controversy, see Craig's "Olden Time," Vol. I, published at Pittsburgh in 1846, and Sparks' "Life and Writings of Washington," Vol. II.

CONTENTS.

	PAGE
Prefatory. By Francis Parkman	*xi*
Biographical Sketch of Henry Bouquet	*xvii*
Introduction	3
Historical Account of the Expedition	29
Reflections on the War with the Savages of N. A.	93
Appendix I—Construction of Forts	137
Appendix II—French Forts ceded to Great Britain	141
Appendix III—Route from Philadelphia to Fort Pitt	148
Appendix IV—Indian Towns on the Ohio River	149
Appendix V—Indian Nations of North America	153

PREFATORY.

THE peace of 1763 was the beginning of a new epoch in the history of this continent. The vast region from the Alleghanies to the Rocky Mountains had been explored, mapped out, and, in good measure, occupied by the French. Their forts, missions, and trading posts—the centers, in some cases, of little colonies—were scattered throughout the Valley of the Mississippi and on the borders of all the Great Lakes. They had gained a controlling influence over the Indians, and by the right of discovery and of colonization they regarded the country as their own. When WOLFE and AMHERST conquered Canada, the vast but frail fabric of French empire in the West crumbled to the dust. An industrial democracy, not a military monarchy married to the hierarchy of Rome, was thenceforth to assume the mighty task of conquering this rich wilderness for civilization.

To

To the Indian tribes, its natural owners, the change was nothing but a disaster. They had held, in a certain sense, the balance of power between the rival colonies of France and England. Both had bid for their friendship, and both competed for the trade with them. The French had been the more successful. Their influence was predominant among all the interior tribes, while many of the border Indians, old allies of the English, had of late abandoned them in favor of their rivals. While the French had usually gained the good will, often the ardent attachment, of the tribes with whom they came in contact, the English, for the most part, had inspired only jealousy and dislike. This dislike was soon changed to the most intense hatred. Lawless traders and equally lawless speculators preyed on the Indians; swarms of squatters invaded the lands of the border tribes, and crowded them from their homes.

No race on earth has a more intense and unyielding individuality than the Indians. To the weakness and vices inseparable from all low degrees of human development, he joins a peculiar reserve and pride. He will not coalesce with superior races, and will not imitate them. When enslaved he dies, kills himself,

kills

kills his master, or runs away. It has been his lot to be often hated, but seldom thoroughly despised. His race has never received a nickname, and he has never served as a subject of amusement. There is some humor in him, but he is too grim a figure to be laughed at. One is almost constrained to admire the inflexible obstinacy with which he clings to his own personality, rejects the advances of civilization, and prefers to die as he has lived.

Such, indeed, is the alternative; and it was after the peace of 1763 that this inexorable sentence of civilization or destruction was first proclaimed over the continent in tones no longer doubtful.

That the Indians understood the crisis it would be rash to affirm; but they felt it without fully understanding it. The result was the great Indian war under PONTIAC. The tribes leagued together and rose to drive the English into the sea. All the small posts of the interior were captured from the English, and the frontiers swept with fire. The two great forts, Detroit and Fort Pitt, alone withstood the assailants, and both were reduced to extremity. PONTIAC himself, with the tribes of the Lakes, beleaguered Detroit, while

while the Delawares and Shawanees, with some of the Wyandottes, laid siege, in their barbarous way, to Fort Pitt, or Pittsburgh. Other bands of the same tribes meanwhile ravaged the frontiers of Pennsylvania, burning houses, murdering settlers, laying waste whole districts, and producing an indescribable distress and consternation.

This is the point where the ensuing narrative begins. Happily for the distracted borders and the distressed garrison, a gallant Swiss officer, HENRY BOUQUET, then commanded at Philadelphia, and he was ordered to march, with what troops he could collect, to the relief of Fort Pitt. A similar attempt had been made, with greater means and with fewer obstacles, to relieve Detroit, and the result had been a deplorable defeat; but BOUQUET, an experienced officer, a man of science and a man of sense, proved himself in every way equal to the emergency. The story of this almost desperate attempt is given in the introductory part of the following narrative. The events recounted in the body of the book belong to the succeeding year. The Indians defeated by BOUQUET at Bushy Run, and foiled by GLADWYN before Detroit, had lost heart and hope. General BRADSTREET led a body
of

Prefatory. xv

of troops up the lakes to force them to a substantial and permanent peace; while BOUQUET, with a similar object, marched into the untrodden wilderness of Ohio. BRADSTREET'S share of the combined expedition was ill-managed, and but partially successful; yet, while failing to do his own part thoroughly, he took it upon himself to accomplish that assigned to his brother commander. BOUQUET rejected his interference, disregarded the unauthorized treaties he had made, and pursued his march with results which the narrative itself will show. I have examined the original documents on which it is based, and can testify that they have been faithfully followed.

The authorship of the "Historical Account of the Expedition against the Ohio Indians," has been ascribed, by Rich, Allibone, and others, to Thomas Hutchins, at that time Geographer of the United States, who supplied the map; but the following extract from a letter of Dr. William Smith, Provost of the College of Philadelphia, dated January 13, 1766, seems a sufficient proof that the credit belongs to him.

"*Mr. Croghan,*" he writes to SIR WILLIAM JOHNSON, "*set out the day before I expected he would, else I
"proposed sending you a copy of 'Bouquet's Expedition
"to Muskingum,' which I drew up from some papers he
"favored*

"*favored me with, and which is reprinted in England,* " *and has had a very favorable reception.*"

Mr. A. R. Spofford, the intelligent custodian of the Library of Congress, first made this contemporary evidence known, having discovered the letter in the Force collection of papers, lately acquired by that Library.

FRANCIS PARKMAN.

BOSTON,
August, 1868.

BIOGRAPHICAL SKETCH

OF

HENRY BOUQUET.

TRANSLATED FROM THE FRENCH EDITION OF THIS WORK PUBLISHED
AT AMSTERDAM IN 1769 BY C. G. F. DUMAS.

HENRY BOUQUET was a man of a fine person, a superior understanding, and a feeling heart. He made no claim to the good opinion of others, neither did he solicit it. All were compelled to esteem him, and hence there were many of his profession who thought they could dispense with loving him. Firmness, intrepidity, calmness, presence of mind in the greatest dangers, virtues so essential in a commander, were natural to him. His presence inspired confidence and impressed respect, encouraged his friends and confounded his foes.

He

He was born at Rolle,* in the canton of Berne, in Switzerland. In 1736, being then seventeen years old, he was received as a cadet in the Regiment of Constant, in the service of LL. HH. PP.,† and in 1738 he obtained the commission of ensign in the same regiment. Thence he passed into that of Roguin, in the service of the KING OF SARDINIA, and distinguished himself first as first lieutenant, and afterward as adjutant, in the memorable and ably-conducted campaigns of the wars which that great prince sustained against the combined forces of France and Spain. At the battle of Cony, being ordered to occupy a piece of ground at the brink of a precipice, he led his men thither in such a way that not one of them saw that they were within two steps of destruction should the enemy force the position. Meanwhile, calmly watching the movements of both armies, he made his soldiers observe, in order to distract their attention, that these movements could be seen much better by the light of the moon than in broad daylight.

---

* Rolle is a small town in the canton of Vaud. Together with the greater part of the Vaudois territory, it was formerly under the government of Berne, and regarded as a part of that canton. It is on the northern borders of the Lake of Geneva.—F. P.

† *Leurs Hautes Puissances*—i. e., The States General of Holland.—F. P.

The

Henry Bouquet. xix

The accounts, no less exact than interesting, which he sent to Holland of the operations of these campaigns, came to the knowledge of His Serene Highness, the late PRINCE OF ORANGE, and induced him to engage this officer in the service of the Republic. In consequence, Mr. BOUQUET entered as captain commandant, with the rank of lieutenant colonel, into the regiment of Swiss Guards, newly formed at the Hague, in 1748, and was immediately chosen to go, jointly with Generals BURMANNIA and CORNABÉ, to receive from the French the places in the Low Countries which they were about to evacuate, and to arrange the return of the prisoners of war which France gave up to the Republic in conformity with the Treaty of Aix-la-Chapelle. A few months after, LORD MIDDLETON invited him to accompany him in his travels in France and Italy.

On his return to the Hague, he devoted every moment which his regimental duties allowed to the careful study of the military art, and above all of mathematics, which are the foundation of it. The intimate relations which he formed with Professors HEMSTERHUIS, KÖNIG, and ALLAMAND, and with several other learned men in every branch of science, greatly

greatly facilitated his acquisition of the thorough knowledge which afterward gave him a yet higher distinction, and caused him to appear with such advantage in the vast theater of the war kindled between France and England in 1754.*

As this war obliged England to send troops to America, it was proposed to raise a corps, under the name of ROYAL AMERICANS, formed of three battalions under one commander, the officers of which were to be indifferently either Americans or foreigners, but in all cases men of capacity and experience.† This plan, favored by the DUKE OF CUMBERLAND, was carried into execution, though altered and mutilated by an opposing faction. Mr. BOUQUET and

---

*BOUQUET always retained his fondness for the society of men of science. When in command at Philadelphia, he formed an intimacy with the botanist BERTRAM.—F. P.

† The "Royal American Regiment" was to consist of four battalions of one thousand men each, the ranks to be filled in great measure from the German and other continental settlers of Pennsylvania and Maryland. Fifty of the officers might be foreign Protestants, but the colonel must be a natural-born subject. See "*Act to enable His Majesty to grant commissions to a certain number of foreign Protestants*," 29 George II., c. V. The first colonel was JOHN, Earl of Loudoun, but Colonels J. STANWIX, JOSEPH DUSSAUX, C. JEFFEREYS, and JAMES PROVOST, commanded the four battalions respectively. See "*Army List.*" The Royal American Regiment is now the Sixtieth Rifles.—F. P.

his

his intimate friend, Mr. HALDIMAND, were the first to whom those charged with it turned their eyes, and they were urged to serve in this brigade as lieutenant colonels. Both had already reached that rank at the Hague, and by a singular freak of fortune, the officer who was to command them in America was their inferior in Europe. This made them hesitate for some time. Nevertheless, at the urgent persuasion of SIR JOSEPH YORKE, and upon a promise being made them that they should be placed immediately, as colonels commandant, on a footing of equality with the colonel-in-chief of the brigade, they were induced to accept the commissions offered them. As soon as their resolution was taken, they were charged to attract into the corps a sufficient number of good officers, both for the engineer and the artillery service. There was no reason to regret that this matter was entrusted to them. Most of these officers were drawn from the armies of the Republic, and they have answered the expectations of those who chose them in a manner which has done honor to both.

I have not entered into a detailed account of the plan which called into existence the brigade of which I have just spoken, for this would have led me too far.

far. I shall content myself with saying, that its origin, and the favor with which it was received, were due to pure accident; but that its happy execution is solely to be ascribed to the discernment of Sir Joseph Yorke, and to his zeal for his country. It is chiefly, then, to him, that the British Empire owes the distinguished services which these brave officers have rendered it.*

To return to Mr. Bouquet: On his arrival in America, his integrity, as well as his great capacity, soon acquired for him a great credit in the Colonies, especially in Pennsylvania and Virginia. Respected by the soldiers, in credit with all who had a share in the internal government of these provinces, universally esteemed and loved, he had but to ask, and he obtained all that it was possible to grant, because it was believed that he asked nothing but what was necessary and proper, and that all would be faithfully employed for the services of the king and the provinces. This good understanding between the civil and military

---

* Major General Sir Joseph Yorke was appointed British Plenipotentiary to the States General in 1751. He had been aid-de-camp to the Duke of Cumberland at the battle of Fontenoy. In 1788 he was raised to the peerage as Baron Dover. He died without issue in 1792.—F. P.

authorities

authorities contributed to his success quite as much as his ability.

Immediately after the conclusion of peace with the Indians, the king made him brigadier general and commandant of his troops in all the Southern Colonies of British America. He died at Pensacola* lamented by his friends and universally regretted. I wish that the Colonies, which I sincerely love, may have a long succession of such defenders. The young officers who read this, will permit me to propose him as a model for their imitation, and an example well fitted to excite in them a noble emulation. It is to his honor that I have undertaken this translation, and it is to his memory that I dedicate it.

[* His death must have occurred in the autumn of 1765, not long after his return from this "*Expedition against the Ohio Indians,*" for, in the *Gentleman's Magazine* (London) for January, 1766, we find the following among the promotions in the British army: "*Aug. Provost, Esq.,* Lieut. Col. of the 60th Reg., in room of H. BOUQUET, dec."]

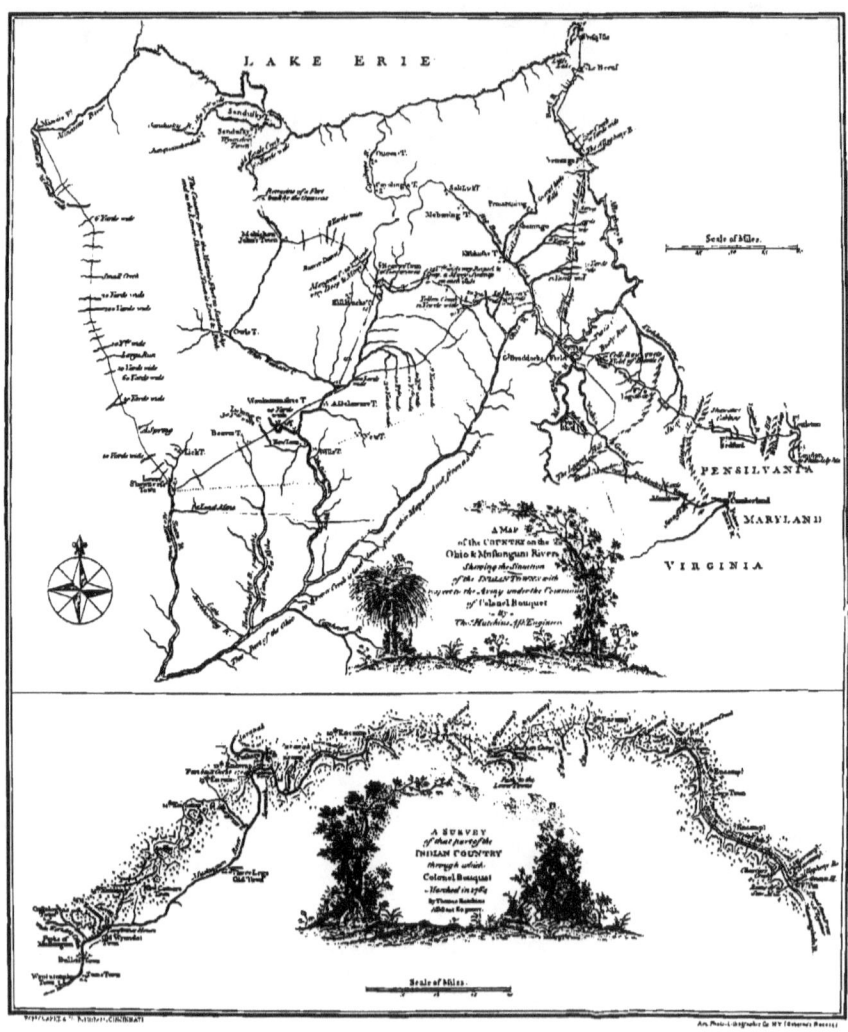

AN HISTORICAL ACCOUNT OF THE EXPEDITION AGAINST THE OHIO INDIANS,

IN THE YEAR MDCCLXIV.

UNDER THE COMMAND OF

HENRY BOUQUET, ESQ.

COLONEL OF FOOT, AND NOW BRIGADIER GENERAL IN AMERICA.

Including his Tranfactions with the INDIANS,
Relative to the DELIVERY of their PRISONERS,
And the PRELIMINARIES of PEACE.

With an INTRODUCTORY ACCOUNT of the Preceding CAMPAIGN,
And BATTLE at BUSHY-RUN.

To which are annexed

MILITARY PAPERS,

CONTAINING

Reflections on the War with the Savages; a Method of forming Frontier Settlements; fome Account of the INDIAN Country; with a Lift of Nations, Fighting Men, Towns, Diftances, and different Routs.

The whole illuftrated with a MAP and COPPER-PLATES.

Publifhed, from authentic Documents, by a Lover of his Country.

PHILADELPHIA, PRINTED:
LONDON, Re-printed for T. JEFFERIES, Geographer to his MAJESTY, at Charing Crofs. MDCCLXVI.

INTRODUCTION.

THE general peace, concluded between Great-Britain, France and Spain, in the year 1762, although viewed in different lights by perfons varioufly affected in the mother country, was neverthelefs univerfally confidered as a moft happy event in America.

To behold the French, who had fo long inftigated and fupported the Indians, in the moft deftructive wars and cruel depredations on our frontier fettlements, at laft compelled to cede all Canada, and reftricted to the weftern fide of Miffifippi, was what we had long wifhed, but fcarcely hoped an accomplifhment of in our own days. The precifion with which our boundaries were expreffed, admitted of no ground for future difputes, and was matter of exultation to every one who underftood and regarded the intereft of thefe colonies. We had now the pleafing profpect of "entire*

---

* The feveral quotations in this introduction are taken from the Annual Regifter, 1763, which is written with great elegance and truth, fo far as the author appears to have been furnifhed with materials.

" fecurity

"fecurity from all moleftation of the Indians, fince French intrigues could no longer be employed to feduce, or French force to fupport them."

" UNHAPPILY, however, we were difappointed in this expectation. Our danger arofe from that very quarter, in which we imagined ourfelves in the moft perfect fecurity; and juft at the time when we concluded the Indians to be entirely awed, and almoft· fubjected by our power, they fuddenly fell upon the frontiers of our moft valuable fettlements, and upon all our out-lying forts, with fuch unanimity in the defign, and with fuch favage fury in the attack, as we had not experienced, even in the hotteft times of any former war."

SEVERAL reafons have been affigned for this perfidious conduct on their part; fuch as an omiffion of the ufual prefents, and fome fettlements made on lands not yet purchafed from them. But thefe caufes, if true, could only affect a few tribes, and never could have formed fo general a combination againft us. The true reafon feems to have been a jealoufy of our growing power, heightened by their feeing the French almoft wholly driven out of America, and a number of forts now poffeffed by us,
which

which commanded the great lakes and rivers communicating with them, and awed the whole Indian country. They probably imagined that they beheld "in every little garrifon the germ of a future "colony," and thought it incumbent on them to make one general and timely effort to crufh our power in the birth.

By the papers in the Appendix, a general idea may be formed of the ftrength of the different Indian nations furrounding our fettlements, and their fituation with refpect to each other.

The Shawanefe, Delawares and other Ohio tribes, took the lead in this war, and feem to have begun it rather too precipitately, before the other tribes in confederacy with them, were ready for action.

Their fcheme appears to have been projected with much deliberate mifchief in the intention, and more than ufual fkill in the fyftem of execution. They were to make one general and fudden attack upon our frontier fettlements in the time of harveft, to deftroy our men, corn, cattle, &c. as far as they could penetrate, and to ftarve our outpofts, by cutting off their fupplies, and all communication with the inhabitants of the Provinces.

In

In purfuance of this bold and bloody project, they fell fuddenly upon our traders whom they had invited into their country, murdered many of them, and made one general plunder of their effects, to an immenfe value.

The frontiers of Pennfylvania, Maryland and Virginia, were immediately over-run with fcalping parties, marking their way with blood and devaftation wherever they came, and all thofe examples of favage cruelty, which never fail to accompany an Indian war.

All our out-forts, even at the remoteft diftances, were attacked about the fame time; and the following ones foon fell into the enemies hands—viz. Le Boeuf, Venango, Prefqu' Ifle, on and near lake Erie; La Bay upon lake Michigan; St. Jofeph's, upon the river of that name; Miamis upon the Miamis river; Ouachtanon upon the Ouabache; Sandufky upon lake Junundat; and Michilimackinac.

Being but weakly garrifoned, trufting to the fecurity of a general peace fo lately eftablifhed, unable to obtain the leaft intelligence from the colonies, or from each other, and being feparately perfuaded

Introduction. 7

perfuaded by their treacherous and favage affailants that they had carried every other place before them, it could not be expected that thefe fmall pofts could hold out long; and the fate of their garrifons is terrible to relate.

THE news of their furrender, and the continued ravages of the enemy, ftruck all America with confternation, and depopulated a great part of our frontiers. We now faw moft of thofe pofts, fuddenly wrefted from us, which had been the great object of the late war, and one of the principal advantages acquired by the peace. Only the forts of Niagara, the Detroit and Fort-Pitt, remained in our hands, of all that had been purchafed with fo much blood and treafure. But thefe were places of confequence, and we hope it ever will remain an argument of their importance, and of the attention that fhould be paid to their future fupport, that they alone continued to awe the whole power of the Indians, and balanced the fate of the war between them and us!

THESE forts, being larger, were better garrifoned and fupplied to ftand a fiege of fome length, than the places that fell. Niagara was not attacked, the enemy judging it too ftrong.

THE

8   *Introduction.*

The officers who commanded the other two deserved the highest honour for the firmness with which they defended them, and the hardships they sustained rather than deliver up places of such importance.

Major Gladwin, in particular, who commanded at the Detroit, had to withstand the united and vigorous attacks of all the nations living upon the Lakes.

The design of this publication, and the materials in my hands, lead me more immediately to speak of the defence and relief of Fort Pitt.

The Indians had early surrounded that place, and cut off all communication from it, even by message. Tho' they had no cannon, nor understood the methods of a regular siege, yet, with incredible boldness, they posted themselves under the banks of both rivers† by the walls of the fort, and continued as it were buried there, from day to day, with astonishing patience; pouring in an incessant storm of musquetry and fire arrows; hoping at length, by famine, by fire, or by harrassing out the garrison, to carry their point.

† The Ohio and Monongahela, at the junction of which stands Fort Pitt.

Captain

Introduction. 9

CAPTAIN ECUYER, who commanded there, tho' he wanted feveral neceffaries for fuftaining a fiege, and the fortifications had been greatly damaged by the floods, took all the precautions which art and judgment could fuggeft for the repair of the place, and repulfing the enemy. His garrifon, joined by the inhabitants, and furviving traders who had taken refuge there, feconded his efforts with refolution. Their fituation was alarming, being remote from all immediate affiftance, and having to deal with an enemy from whom they had no mercy to expect.

GENERAL AMHERST, the commander in chief, not being able to provide in time for the fafety of the remote pofts, bent his chief attention to the relief of the Detroit, Niagara, and Fort-Pitt. The communication with the two former was chiefly by water, from the province of New-York; and it was on that account the more eafy to throw fuccours into them. The detachment fent to the Detroit arrived there on the 29th of July, 1763; but Captain Dalyell, who commanded that detachment, and feventy of his men, loft their lives in a rencounter with the Indians near the fort. Previous to this difafter he had paffed thro' Niagara, and left a reinforcement there.

FORT

FORT PITT remained all this while in a moſt critical ſituation. No account could be obtained from the garriſon, nor any relief ſent to it, but by a long and tedious land march of near 200 miles beyond the ſettlements; and through thoſe dangerous paſſes where the fate of Braddock and others ſtill riſes on the imagination.

COL. BOUQUET was appointed to march to the relief of this fort, with a large quantity of military ſtores and proviſions, eſcorted by the ſhattered remainder of the 42d and 77th regiments, lately returned in a diſmal condition from the Weſt-Indies, and far from being recovered of their fatigues at the ſiege of the Havannah. General Amherſt, having at that time no other troops to ſpare, was obliged to employ them in a ſervice which would have required men of the ſtrongeſt conſtitution and vigour.

EARLY orders had been given to prepare a convoy of proviſions on the frontiers of Pennſylvania, but ſuch were the univerſal terror and conſternation of the inhabitants, that when Col. BOUQUET arrived at Carliſle, nothing had yet been done. A great number of the plantations had been plundered and burnt, by the ſavages; many

of

of the mills deftroyed, and the full-ripe crops ftood waving in the field, ready for the fickle, but the reapers were not to be found!

THE greateft part of the county of Cumberland, thro' which the army had to pafs, was deferted, and the roads were covered with diftreffed families, flying from their fettlements, and deftitute of all the neceffaries of life.

IN the midft of that general confufion, the fupplies neceffary for the expedition became very precarious, nor was it lefs difficult to procure horfes and carriages for the ufe of the troops.

THE commander found that, inftead of expecting fuch fupplies from a miferable people, he himfelf was called by the voice of humanity to beftow on them fome fhare of his own provifions to relieve their prefent exigency. However, in 18 days after his arrival at Carlifle, by the prudent and active meafures which he purfued, joined to his knowledge of the country, and the diligence of the perfons he employed, the convoy and carriages were procured with the affiftance of the interior parts of the country, and the army proceeded.

THEIR

Their march did not abate the fears of the dejected inhabitants. They knew the ftrength and ferocity of the enemy. They remembered the former defeats even of our beft troops, and were full of diffidence and apprehenfions on beholding the fmall number and fickly ftate of the regulars employed in this expedition. Without the leaft hopes, therefore, of fuccefs, they feemed only to wait for the fatal event, which they dreaded, to abandon all the country beyond the Sufquehannah.

In fuch defpondency of mind, it is not furprifing, that tho' their whole was at ftake, and depended intirely upon the fate of this little army, none of them offered to affift in the defence of the country, by joining the expedition; in which they would have been of infinite fervice, being in general well acquainted with the woods, and excellent markfmen.

It cannot be contefted that the defeat of the regular troops on this occafion, would have left the province of Pennfylvania in particular, expofed to the moft imminent danger, from a victorious, daring, and barbarous enemy; for (excepting the frontier people of Cumberland county) the bulk

of

Introduction. 13

of its induftrious inhabitants is compofed of merchants, tradefmen and farmers, unaccuftomed to arms, and without a militia law.

THE legiflature ordered, indeed, 700 men to be raifed for the protection of the frontiers during the harveft; but what dependence could be placed in raw troops, newly raifed and undifciplined? Under fo many difcouraging circumftances, the Colonel (deprived of all affiftance from the provinces, and having none to expect from the General, who had fent him the laft man that could be removed from the hofpitals) had nothing elfe to truft to, but about 500 foldiers of approved courage and refolution indeed, but infirm, and intire ftrangers to the woods, and to this new kind of war. A number of them were even fo weak, as not to be able to march, and fixty were carried in waggons to reinforce the garrifons of the fmall pofts on the communication.

MEANWHILE Fort-Ligonier, fituated beyond the Allegheny-Mountains, was in the greateft danger of falling into the hands of the enemy, before the army could reach it. The ftockade being very bad, and the garrifon extremely weak, they had attacked it vigoroufly, but had been repulfed by the bravery

bravery and good conduct of Lieutenant Blane who commanded there.

THE prefervation of that poft was of the utmoft confequence, on account of its fituation and the quantity of military ftores it contained, which if the enemy could have got poffeffion of, would have enabled them to continue their attack upon Fort-Pitt, and reduced the army to the greateft ftreights. For an object of that importance, every rifk was to be run; and the Colonel determined to fend through the woods, with proper guides, a party of thirty men to join that garrifon. They fucceeded by forced marches in that hazardous attempt, not having been difcovered by the enemy till they came within fight of the Fort, into which they threw themfelves, after receiving fome running fhot.

PREVIOUS to that reinforcement of regulars, 20 voluntiers, all good woodfmen, had been fent to Fort-Ligonier by Capt. Ourry, who commanded at Fort-Bedford another very confiderable magazine of provifions, and military ftores, the principal and centrical ftage between Carlifle and Fort-Pitt, being about 100 miles diftance from each. This fort was alfo in a ruinous condition, and very weakly garrifoned, although the two fmall
intermediate

intermediate pofts, at the croffings of the Juniata and of Stony Creek, had been abandoned to ftrengthen it.

HERE the diftreffed families, fcattered for 12 or 15 miles round, fled for protection, leaving moft of their effects a prey to the favages.

ALL the neceffary precautions were taken by the commanding officer, to prevent furprize, and repel open force, as alfo to render ineffectual the enemies fire arrows. He armed all the fighting men, who formed two companies of voluntiers, and did duty with the garrifon till the arrival of two companies of light infantry, detached as foon as poffible from Colonel Bouquet's little army.

THESE two magazines being fecured, the Colonel advanced to the remoteft verge of our fettlements, where he could receive no fort of intelligence of the number, pofition, or motions of the enemy. Not even at Fort-Bedford, where he arrived with his whole convoy on the 25th of July, for tho' the Indians did not attempt to attack the fort, they had by this time killed, fcalped, and taken eighteen perfons in that neighborhood, and their fculking parties were fo fpread, that at laft no exprefs could efcape escape them. " This" (want of intelligence) "is " often a very embarrassing circumstance in the con- " duct of a campaign in America. The Indians " had better intelligence, and no sooner were they " informed of the march of our Army, than they " broke up the siege of Fort-Pitt, and took the " rout by which they knew we were to proceed, " resolved to take the first advantageous oppor- " tunity of an attack on the march."

(In this uncertainty of intelligence under which the Colonel laboured, he marched from Fort-Bedford the 28th of July, and as soon as he reached Fort-Ligonier, he determined very prudently to leave his waggons at that post, and to proceed only with the pack horses. Thus disburdened, the army continued their rout. Before them lay a dangerous defile at Turtle Creek, several miles in length, commanded the whole way by high and craggy hills. This defile he intended to have passed the ensuing night, by a double or forced march; thereby, if possible, to elude the vigilance of so elert an enemy, proposing only to make a short halt in his way, to refresh the Troops, at Bushy-Run,)

(When they came within half a mile of that place, about one in the afternoon, (August 5th, 1763) after

Introduction.

after an harraffing march of feventeen miles, and juft as they were expecting to relax from their fatigue, they were fuddenly attacked by the Indians, on their advanced guard; which being fpeedily and firmly fupported, the enemy was beat off, and even purfued to a confiderable diftance.

'† BUT the flight of thefe barbarians muft often
' be confidered as a part of the engagement, (if we
' may ufe the expreffion) rather than a dereliction
' of the field. The moment the purfuit ended,
' they returned with renewed vigour to the attack.
' Several other parties, who had been in ambufh in
' fome high grounds which lay along the flanks of
' the army, now ftarted up at once, and falling with
' a refolution equal to that of their companions,
' galled our troops with a moft obftinate fire.

' IT was neceffary to make a general charge with
' the whole line to diflodge them from thefe heights.
' This charge fucceeded; but ftill the fuccefs pro-
' duced no decifive advantage; for as foon as the

† The above quotation is from the writer already mentioned, and feems fo accurately and elegantly drawn up, from the account of this engagement, fent to his Majefty's minifters, that nothing better can be inferted in its room. There are but one or two fmall miftakes in it, which are here corrected.

' favages

'favages were driven from one poft, they ftill ap-
'peared on another, till by conftant reinforcements
'they were at length able to furround the whole
'detachment, and attack the convoy which had
'been left in the rear.

'This manœuvre obliged the main body to
'fall back in order to protect it. The action,
'which grew every moment hotter and hotter,
'now became general. Our troops were attacked
'on every fide; the favages fupported their fpirit
'throughout; but the fteady behaviour of the
'Englifh troops, who were not thrown in the leaft
'confufion by the very difcouraging nature of this
'fervice, in the end prevailed; they repulfed the
'enemy, and drove them from all their pofts with
'fixed bayonets.

'The engagement ended only with the day,
'having continued from one without any inter-
'miffion.

'The ground, on which the action ended, was
'not altogether inconvenient for an encampment.
'The convoy and the wounded were in the middle,
'and the troops, difpofed in a circle, incompaffed
'the whole. In this manner, and with little
'repofe,

'repofe, they paffed an anxious night, obliged to
'the ftricteft vigilance by an enterprizing enemy
'who had furrounded them.)

('THOSE who have only experienced the feverities
'and dangers of a campaign in Europe, can fcarcely
'form an idea of what is to be done and endured
'in an American war. To act in a country cul-
'tivated and inhabited, where roads are made,
'magazines are eftablifhed, and hofpitals provided;
'where there are good towns to retreat to in cafe of
'misfortune; or, at the worft, a generous enemy
'to yield to, from whom no confolation, but the
'honour of victory, can be wanting; this may be
'confidered as the exercife of a fpirited and adven-
'turous mind, rather than a rigid conteft where all
'is at ftake, and mutual deftruction the object:
'and as a contention between rivals for glory,
'rather than a real ftruggle between fanguinary
'enemies. But in an American campaign every
'thing is terrible; the face of the country, the
'climate, the enemy. There is no refrefhment fo r
'the healthy, nor relief for the fick. A vaft un-
'hofpitable defart, unfafe and treacherous, fur-
'rounds them, where victories are not decifive, but
'defeats are ruinous; and fimple death is the leaft
'misfortune which can happen to them. This

'forms

'forms a service truly critical, in which all the
'firmness of the body and mind is put to the se-
'verest trial; and all the exertions of courage and
'address are called out. If the actions of these
'rude campaigns are of less dignity, the adven-
'tures in them are more interesting to the heart,
'and more amusing to the imagination, than the
'events of a regular war.)

('But to return to the party of English, whom
'we left in the woods. At the first dawn of light
'the savages began to declare themselves, all about
'the camp, at the distance of about 500 yards; and
'by shouting and yelling in the most horrid man-
'ner, quite round that extensive circumference, en-
'deavoured to strike terror by an ostentation of
'their numbers, and their ferocity.

'After this alarming preparative, they attacked
'our forces, and, under the favour of an incessant
'fire, made several bold attempts to penetrate into
'the camp. They were repulsed in every attempt,
'but by no means discouraged from new ones.
'Our troops, continually victorious, were contin-
'ually in danger. They were besides extremely
'fatigued with a long march, and with the equally
'long action, of the preceding day; and they were
'distressed

'diftreffed to the laft degree by a total want of water,
' much more intolerable than the enemy's fire.

' TIED to their convoy, they could not lofe fight
' of it for a moment, without expofing, not only
' that interefting object, but their wounded men,
' to fall a prey to the favages, who preffed them on
' every fide. To move was impracticable. Many
' of the horfes were loft, and many of the drivers,
' ftupefied by their fears, hid themfelves in the
' bufhes, and were incapable of hearing or obeying
' orders.

' THEIR fituation became extremely critical and
' perplexing, having experienced that the moft
' lively efforts made no impreffion upon an enemy,
' who always gave way when preffed; but who, the
' moment the purfuit was over, returned with as
' much alacrity as ever to the attack. Befieged
' rather than engaged; attacked without interrup-
' tion, and without decifion; able neither to ad-
' vance nor to retreat, they faw before them the
' moft melancholy profpect of crumbling away by
' degrees, and entirely perifhing without revenge
' or honour, in the midft of thofe dreadful defarts.
' The fate of Braddock was every moment before
' their eyes; but they were more ably conducted.

'THE

'The commander was senfible that every thing 'depended upon bringing the favages to a clofe 'engagement, and to ftand their ground when at-'tacked. Their audacioufnefs, which had increafed 'with their fuccefs, feemed favourable to this 'defign. He endeavoured, therefore, to increafe 'their confidence as much as poffible.

'For that purpofe he contrived the following 'ftratagem. Our troops were pofted on an emi-'nence, and formed a circle round their convoy 'from the preceding night, which order they ftill 'retained. Col. Bouquet gave directions, that 'two companies of his troops, who had been 'pofted in the moft advanced fituations, fhould 'fall within the circle; the troops on the right 'and left immediately opened their files, and filled 'up the vacant fpace, that they might feem to 'cover their retreat. Another company of light 'infantry, with one of grenadiers, were ordered '"to lie in ambufcade," to fupport the two 'firft companies of grenadiers, who moved on 'the feigned retreat, and were intended to begin 'the real attack. The difpofitions were well 'made, and the plan executed without the leaft 'confufion.

'The

Introduction.

'THE favages gave entirely into the fnare. The
'thin line of troops, which took poffeffion of the
'ground which the two companies of light foot had
'left, being brought in nearer to the center of the
'circle, the barbarians miftook thofe motions for a
'retreat, abandoned the woods which covered them,
'hurried headlong on, and advancing with the moft
'daring intrepidity, galled the Englifh troops with
'their heavy fire. But at the very moment when,
'certain of fuccefs, they thought themfelves mafters
'of the camp, the two firft companies made a fud-
'den turn, and fallying out from a part of the hill,
'which could not be obferved, fell furioufly upon
'their right flank.

'THE favages, though they found themfelves
'difappointed and expofed, preferved their recol-
'lection, and refolutely returned the fire which
'they had received. Then it was the fuperiority
'of combined ftrength and difcipline appeared.
'On the fecond charge they could no longer fuftain
'the irrefiftible fhock of the regular troops, who
'rufhing upon them, killed many, and put the reft
'to flight.

'AT the inftant when the favages betook them-
'felves to flight, the other two companies, which
'had

' had been ordered to fupport the firft, rofe "from
' "ambufcade," marched to the enemy, and gave
' them their full fire. This accomplifhed their de-
' feat. The four companies now united, did not
' give them time to look behind them, but purfued
' the enemy till they were totally difperfed.

'THE other bodies of the favages attempted
' nothing. They were kept in awe during the
' engagement by the reft of the Britifh troops, who
' were fo pofted as to be ready to fall on them
' upon the leaft motion. Having been witneffes
' to the defeat of their companions, without any
' effort to fupport or affift them, they at length
' followed their example and fled.

' THIS judicious and fuccefsful manœuvre refcued
' the party from the moft imminent danger. The
' victory fecured the field, and cleared all the adja-
' cent woods. But ftill the march was fo difficult,
' and the army had fuffered fo much, and fo many
' horfes were loft, that before they were able to pro-
' ceed, they were reluctantly obliged to deftroy fuch
' part of their convoy of provifions as they could
' not carry with them for want of horfes. Being
' lightened by this facrifice, they proceeded to
' Bufhy-Run, where finding water, they encamped.')

A

PLAN OF THE BATTLE NEAR BUSHY-RUN,

Gained by Colonel Bouquet, over the
Delawares, Shawanefe, Mingoes, Wyandots, Mohikons, Miamies, & Ottawas;
on the 5th and 6th of August 1763.
Survey'd by Thos. Hutchins, *Assistant Engineer.*

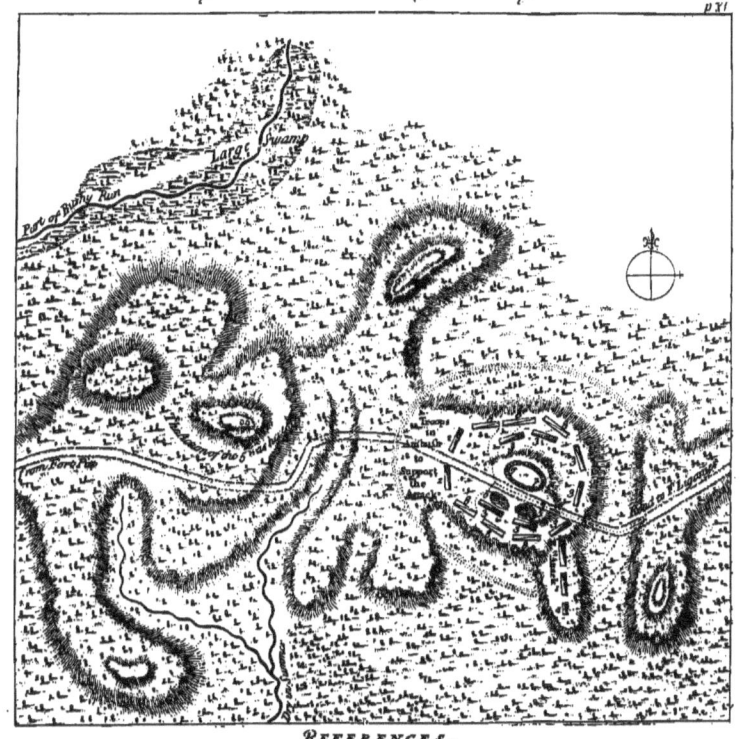

REFERENCES.

1. Grenadiers
2. Light Infantry
3. Battalion Men
4. Rangers
5. Cattle
6. Horses
7. Entrenchment of Bags for the Wounded
x. The Enemy
8. First Position of the Troops
o o Graves

Introduction. 25

A PLAN of this engagement is annexed, and it was thought the more neceſſary here to inſert a particular account of it, as the new manœuvres† and ſkilful conduct of the commander, ſeem to have been the principal means, not only of preſerving his army in the moſt critical ſituation, but likewiſe of enſuring them a compleat victory.

THE enemy loſt about ſixty men on this occaſion, ſome of them their chief warriors; which they reputed a very ſevere ſtroke. They had likewiſe many wounded in the purſuit. The Engliſh loſt about fifty men and had about ſixty wounded.

THE ſavages, thus ſignally defeated in all their attempts to cut off this reinforcement upon its march, began to retreat with the utmoſt precipitation to their remote ſettlements, wholly giving up their deſigns againſt Fort-Pitt; at which place Col. Bouquet arrived ſafe with his convoy, four

† Another reaſon for being ſo particular in this account, is that the military papers annexed to this work, and the plan for carrying on any future war with the Indians, were compoſed upon the experience of this engagement, by an officer long employed in the ſervice he deſcribes. His own improvement was his principal motive in the compoſition of them; but being told that they might convey many uſeful hints to others, and be of much ſervice if laid before the public, he was pleaſed, upon my requeſt, freely to communicate them to me for that purpoſe.

days

days after the action; receiving no further molestation on the road, except a few scattered shot from a disheartened and flying enemy.

Here the Colonel was obliged to put an end to the operations of this campaign, not having a sufficient force to pursue the enemy beyond the Ohio and take advantage of the victory obtained over them; nor having any reason to expect a timely reinforcement from the provinces in their distressed situation. He was therefore forced to content himself with supplying Fort-Pitt, and other places on the communication, with provisions, ammunition, and stores; stationing his small army to the best advantage he could, against the approach of winter.

The transactions of the succeeding campaign, will be the subject of the following work, and we shall conclude this introduction, by shewing the sense which his Majesty was pleased to entertain, of the conduct and bravery of the officers and army, on this trying occasion.

Head-Quarters,

HEAD-QUARTERS, NEW-YORK, Jan. 5, 1764.

ORDERS.

"HIS Majefty has been gracioufly pleafed to
"fignify to the commander in chief, his
"royal approbation of the conduct and bravery of
"Col. BOUQUET, and the officers and troops under
"his command, in the two actions of the 5th and
"6th of Auguft; in which, notwithftanding the
"many circumftances of difficulty and diftrefs they
"laboured under, and the unufual fpirit and refo-
"lution of the Indians, they repelled and defeated
"the repeated attacks of the Savages, and con-
"ducted their convoy fafe to Fort-Pitt.
"Signed   MONCREIF,
"Major of Brigade."
To Colonel BOUQUET,
or officer commanding at Fort-Pitt.

AN

HISTORICAL ACCOUNT

OF

COLONEL BOUQUET's EXPEDITION

AGAINST THE OHIO INDIANS IN THE YEAR 1764.

IN the preceding introduction, fome account hath been given of the fudden, treacherous and unprovoked attack, made by the Indians upon the frontiers of Pennfylvania, Maryland, and Virginia, foon after the publication of the general Peace, at a time when we were but juft beginning to refpire from our former calamities, and looked for an approach of quiet on every fide. The principal tranfactions of the campaign 1763 have likewife been briefly recapitulated, and the reader informed by what means the editor became
poffeffed

poffeffed of the valuable papers, which have enabled him to bring the hiftory of this Indian war to a conclufion, and furnifhed the materials of the following fheets.

Colonel Bouquet, as before mentioned, not having a fufficient number of troops to garrifon the different pofts, under his command, and at the fame time to crofs the Ohio and take advantage of the dejection into which he had thrown the enemy, by the defeat at Bufhy-Run, was obliged to reftrain his operations to the fupplying the forts with provifions, ammunition and other neceffaries.

In the execution of this fervice, he received no annoyance from the enemy, for they now faw themfelves not only forced to give up their defigns againft Fort-Pitt; but, retreating beyond the Ohio, they deferted their former towns, and abandoned all the country between Prefque-Ifle and Sandufki; not thinking themfelves fafe till they arrived at Mufkingam.

Here they began to form new fettlements, and remained quiet during the winter. But, in the mean time, having fupplied themfelves with powder, &c. from the French traders, (and now

flattering

Colonel Bouquet's Expedition. 31

flattering themfelves that the great diftance of their fettlements would render them inacceffible to our troops) the enfuing fpring 1764 prefented thefe favage enemies afrefh on our frontiers ; ravaging and murdering with their ufual barbarity.

To chaftife them for their perfidy, General Gage refolved to attack them on two different fides, and to force them from our frontiers ; by carrying the war into the heart of their own country. With this view, he deftined a corps of troops to proceed under Col. Bradftreet, to act againft the Wiandots, Ottawas, Chipwas and other nations, living upon or near the lakes ; while another corps, under the command of Col. Bouquet, fhould attack the Delawares, Shawanefe, Mingoes, Mohickons, and other nations, between the Ohio and the lakes.

THESE two corps were to act in concert ; and as that of Col. Bradftreet could be ready much fooner than the other, he was to proceed to Detroit, Michilimackinac and other places. On his return he was to encamp and remain at Sandufki, to awe, by that pofition, the numerous tribes of weftern Indians, fo as to prevent their fending any affift-ance to the Ohio Indians, while Colonel Bouquet
fhould

should execute his plan of attacking them in the heart of their settlements.

Col. Bouquet's expedition was to proceed altogether by land, and was on that account attended with great difficulties. His men were to penetrate through a continued depth of woods, and a savage unexplored country; without roads, without posts, and without a retreat if they failed of success. When once engaged in these deserts, they had no convoy, nor any kind of assistance to expect. Every thing was to be carried with them — their ammunition, baggage, tools, stores, and provisions necessary for the troops during the whole expedition. And besides, they were liable to many embarrasments, and difficulties which no prudence could foresee, scarce any caution prevent; so that, in this account, sundry things, which, in the usual method of conducting military operations, might not be thought worthy of detail, may neverthelefs be found highly serviceable to those who may afterwards be employed in this species of war, which is new to Europeans, who must submit to be instructed in it by experience, and in many articles even by the savages themselves.

Part of the 42d and 60th regiments were ordered

Colonel Bouquet's Expedition. 33

ordered on this expedition, and were to be joined by two hundred friendly Indians, and the troops required of Virginia and Pennſylvania. The Indians never came, and the Virginians pleaded their inability to raiſe men, having already in pay about 700 militia for the defence of their own frontier. In Pennſylvania, a bill for raiſing 1000 men was paſſed May 30th; but, with the utmoſt diligence that could be uſed, the number could not be compleated till the beginning of Auguſt.

On the 5th of that month, the men being aſſembled at Carliſle, one hundred and eighteen miles to the weſtward of Philadelphia, Governor Penn, who had accompanied Col. Bouquet to that place, acquainted the two Pennſylvania battalions with the neceſſity we were laid under of chaſtiſing the Indians " for their repeated and unprovoked
" barbarities on the inhabitants of the Province ;
" a juſt reſentment of which, added to a remem-
" brance of the loyalty and courage of our pro-
" vincial troops on former occaſions, he did not
" doubt, would animate them to do honour to
" their country ; and that they could not but hope
" to be crowned with ſucceſs, as they were to be
" united with the ſame regular troops, and under the
" ſame

" fame able commander, who had by themselves,
" on that very day, the memorable 5th of Auguſt
" in the preceding year, fuſtained the repeated
" attacks of the favages, and obtained a compleat
" victory over them." — He alfo reminded them
" of the exemplary puniſhments that would be
" inflicted on the grievous crime of defertion, if
" any of them were capable of fo far forgetting
" their folemn oath and duty to their king and
" country, as to be involved in it."

COL. BOUQUET then aſſumed the command of the regular and provincial troops; and the four following days were ſpent in the neceſſary preparations for their march; the Colonel giving the moſt exprefs orders to the officers and men to obſerve ſtrict difcipline, and not to commit the leaſt violation of the civil rights or peace of the inhabitants.— He, at the fame time, made the moſt prudent regulations for a fafe and commodious carriage of the baggage, taking care to rid himſelf of all unneceſſary incumbrances.

THE 13th of Auguſt this fmall army got to Fort Loudoun; but notwithſtanding all the precautions taken to prevent defertion, the Pennfylvania troops

troops were now reduced to about 700 men. The Colonel was therefore under a neceffity to apply to the government of that province to enable him to compleat their number to the full complement; which was generoufly granted by a refolve of the Governor and Commiffioners Auguft 16th; and the army advancing now beyond the fettled parts of Pennfylvania, he made application to the colony of Virginia, where (under the countenance of Governor Fauquier) the men wanted were foon raifed, and joined the army at Pittfburg, about the latter end of September.

NOTHING material happened in their march, from Fort Loudoun to Fort Pitt, (formerly Fort Du Quefne) on the Ohio, three hundred and twenty miles weft from Philadelphia; at which place Col. Bouquet arrived the 17th of September.

During this interval, feveral large convoys were forwarded under ftrong efcorts; and though the enemy continued their ravages all that time on the frontiers, they durft not attack any of thofe convoys, which all arrived fafe at Fort Pitt.

WHILE Col. Bouquet was at Fort Loudoun, he
received

received difpatches by exprefs from Colonel Bradftreet, dated from Prefque-Ifle Auguft 14th, acquainting him that he (Colonel Bradftreet) had concluded a peace with the Delawares and Shawanefe; but Colonel Bouquet perceiving clearly that they were not fincere in their intentions, as they continued their murders and depredations, he determined to profecute his plan without remiffion, till he fhould receive further inftructions from General Gage; who, upon the fame principles, refufed to ratify the treaty, and renewed his orders to both armies to attack the enemy.

About the time of Colonel Bouquet's arrival at Fort Pitt, ten Indians appeared on the north fide of the Ohio, defiring a conference; which ftratagem the favages had made ufe of before, to obtain intelligence of our numbers and intentions. Three of the party confented, though with apparent reluctance, to come over to the Fort; and as they could give no fatisfactory reafon for their vifit, they were detained as fpies, and their affociates fled back to their towns.

On the 20th of September Colonel Bouquet fent one of the above three Indians after them with

with a meſſage, in ſubſtance as follows— "I have
"received an account from Colonel Bradſtreet
"that your nations had begged for peace, which he
"had conſented to grant, upon aſſurance that you
"had recalled all your warriors from our frontiers ;
"and in conſequence thereof, I would not have
"proceeded againſt your towns, if I had not heard
"that, in open violation of your engagements, you
"have ſince murdered ſeveral of our people.

"As ſoon as the reſt of the army joins me,
"which I expect immediately, I was therefore de-
"termined to have attacked you, as a people whoſe
"promiſes can no more be relied on. But I will
"put it once more in your power to ſave your-
"ſelves and your families from total deſtruction, by
"giving us ſatisfaction for the hoſtilities committed
"againſt us. And firſt you are to leave the path
"open for my expreſſes from hence to Detroit ;
"and as I am now to ſend two men with diſpatches
"to Colonel Bradſtreet who commands on the
"lakes, I deſire to know whether you will ſend two
"of your people with them to bring them ſafe
"back with an anſwer? And if they receive any
"injury either in going or coming, or if the letters
"are taken from them, I will immediately put the
"Indians

"Indians now in my power to death, and will shew
"no mercy for the future to any of your nations
"that shall fall into my hands. I allow you ten
"days to have my letters delivered at Detroit, and
"ten days to bring me back an answer."

He added "that he had lately had it in his
"power, while they remained on the other side of
"the river, to have put their whole party to death,
"which punishment they had deserved by their
"former treachery; and that if they did not
"improve the clemency now offered to them, by
"returning back as soon as possible with all their
"prisoners, they might expect to feel the full
"weight of a just vengeance and resentment."—

We have been the more particular in our account of this first transaction with the Indians; because the Colonel's firm and determined conduct in opening the campaign, had happy effects in the prosecution of it, and shews by what methods these faithless savages are to be best reduced to reason.

On the 1st of October, two of the Six Nation tribes, an Onondago and Oneida Indian, came to Fort Pitt, and under colour of our ancient friendship

friendſhip with them, and their pretended regard to the Engliſh, endeavored to diſſuade the Colonel from proceeding with the army. They told him that his force was not ſufficient to withſtand the power of the numerous nations through whoſe country he was to paſs, and aſſured him that if he would wait a little, they would all come and make peace with him; at the ſame time recommending it particularly to him to ſend back the two Indians detained as ſpies. Theſe little arts being clearly made uſe of to ſpin out the ſeaſon till the approach of winter ſhould render it impoſſible to proceed, they made but little impreſſion. He told them that he could not depend on the promiſes of the Delawares and Shawaneſe; and was determined to proceed to Tuſcarowas, where, if they had any thing to ſay, he would hear them.

In the mean time, he was uſing the utmoſt diligence to prepare for his march, and was obliged to enforce the ſevereſt diſcipline. One woman belonging to each corps, and two nurſes for the general hoſpital, were all that were permitted to follow the army. The other women in the camp, and thoſe unneceſſary in the garriſon, were ordered immediately down the country into the ſettlements.

Two

Two foldiers were fhot for defertion ; an example which became abfolutely neceffary to fupprefs a crime which, in fuch an expedition, would have been attended with fatal confequences, by weakening an army already too fmall.

Colonel Bouquet, having at length, with great difficulty, collected his troops, formed his magazines, and provided for the fafety of the pofts he was to leave behind him, was ready on the 2d of October to proceed from Fort Pitt, with about 1500 men, including drivers and other neceffary followers of the army.

As a juft idea of the conduct of this expedition, and the great caution taken to prevent furprize, will be beft obtained from the order of march, we fhall here infert it, with a Copper Plate for the illuftration of it, and an accurate Draught, taken from actual furveys, of the road and adjacent country, through which the army paffed.

The Colonel, expreffing the greateft confidence in the bravery of the troops, told them, " he did " not doubt but this war would foon be ended " under God, to their own honor, and the
" future

"future fafety of their country, provided the men
"were ftrictly obedient to orders, and guarded
"againft the furprizes and fudden attacks of a
"treacherous enemy, who never dared to face Britifh
"troops in an open field ; that the diftance of the
"enemy's towns, and the clearing roads to them,
"muft neceffarily require a confiderable time; that
"the troops in thofe deferts, had no other fupplies
"to expect but the ammunition and provifions
"they carried with them ; and that therefore the
"utmoft care and frugality would be neceffary in
"the ufe of them." He publifhed the fevereft
penalties againft thofe who fhould be found guilty
of ftealing or embezzling any part of them, and
ordered his March in the following manner.—

A CORPS of Virginia* volunteers advanced before the whole; detaching three fcouting parties.
One of them, furnifhed with a guide, marched in
the center path, which the army was to follow.
The other two extended themfelves in a line
a-breaft, on the right and left of the aforefaid party,
to reconnoitre the woods.

* Thefe were the men raifed in Virginia to compleat the Pennfylvania troops, and were in the pay of the laft mentioned province.

UNDER

UNDER cover of this corps, the ax-men, confift-
ing of all the artificers, and two companies o
light infantry, followed in three divifions, under
the direction of the chief engineer, to clear three
different paths, in which the troops and the convoy followed, viz.—

THE front-face of the fquare, compofed of part
of the 42d regiment, marched in a column, two
deep, in the center path.

THE right face of the fquare, compofed of the
remainder of the 42d and of the 60th regiment,
marched in a fingle file in the right-hand path.

THE firft battalion of Pennfylvanians compofed
the left face, marching in like manner in the path
to the left of the center.

THE corps de referve, compofed of two platoons
of grenadiers, followed the right and left faces of
the fquare.

THE 2d battalion of Pennfylvanians formed the
rear face of the fquare, and followed the corps de
referve, each in a fingle file, on the right and left
hand

hand paths; all thefe troops covering the convoy, which moved in the center path.

A PARTY of light horfe-men marched behind the rear-face of the fquare, followed by another corps of Virginia volunteers, forming the rear-guard.

THE Pennfylvania volunteers, dividing themfelves equally, and marching in a fingle file, at a proper diftance, flanked the right and left faces of the fquare.

THIS was the general order of march. Nor was lefs attention paid to particular matters of a fubordinate nature. The ammunition and tools were placed in the rear of the firft column, or front face of the fquare, followed by the officers' baggage, and tents. The oxen and fheep came after the baggage, in feparate droves, properly guarded. The provifions came next to the baggage, in four divifions, or brigades of pack-horfes, each conducted by a horfe mafter.

THE troops were ordered to obferve the moft profound filence, and the men to march at two yards diftance from one another. When the line

or

or any part of it halted, the whole were to face outwards; and if attacked on their march, they were to halt immediately, ready to form the fquare when ordered. The light horfe were then to march into the fquare, with the cattle, provifions, ammunition and baggage. Proper difpofitions were likewife made in cafe of an attack in the night; and for encampments, guards, communications between the centries, fignals, and the like.

THINGS being thus fettled, the army decamped from Fort-Pitt on Wednefday October 3d, and marched about one mile and an half over a rich level country, with ftately timber, to camp No. 2. a ftrong piece of ground, pleafantly fituated, with plenty of water and food for cattle.

THURSDAY October 4th, having proceeded about two miles, they came to the Ohio, at the beginning of the narrows, and from thence followed the courfe of the river along a flat gravelly beech, about fix miles and a quarter; with two iflands on their left, the lowermoft about fix miles long, with a rifing ground running acrofs, and gently floping on both fides to its banks, which are high and upright. At the lower end of this ifland, the army left the river, marching through good

good land, broken with fmall hollows to camp No. 3; this day's march being nine miles and a quarter. —

FRIDAY October 5th. In this day's march the army paffed through Loggs-town, fituated feventeen miles and an half, fifty feven perches, by the path, from Fort-Pitt. This place was noted before the laft war for the great trade carried on there by the Englifh and French; but its inhabitants, the Shawanefe and Delawares, abandoned it in the year 1750. The lower town extended about fixty perches over a rich bottom to the foot of a low fteep ridge, on the fummit of which, near the declivity, ftood the upper town, commanding a moft agreeable profpect over the lower, and quite acrofs the Ohio, which is about 500 yards wide here, and by its majeftic eafy current adds much to the beauty of the place. Proceeding beyond Logg's-town, through a fine country, interfperfed with hills and rich valleys, watered by many rivulets, and covered with ftately timber, they came to camp No. 4; on a level piece of ground, with a thicket in the rear, a fmall precipice round the front, with a run of water at the foot, and good food for cattle. This day's march was nine miles, one half, and fifty three perches.

SATURDAY

SATURDAY October 6th, at about three miles diftance from this camp, they came again to the Ohio, purfuing its courfe half a mile farther, and then turning off, over a fteep ridge, they croffed Big Beaver-creek, which is twenty perches wide, the ford ftony and pretty deep. It runs through a rich vale, with a pretty ftrong current, its banks high, the upland adjoining it very good, the timber tall and young. ——— About a mile below its confluence with the Ohio, ftood formerly a large town, on a fteep bank, built by the French of fquare logs, with ftone chimneys, for fome of the Shawanefe, Delaware and Mingo tribes, who abandoned it in the year 1758, when the French deferted Fort Du Quefne. Near the fording of Beaver-creek alfo ftood about feven houfes, which were deferted and deftroyed by the Indians, after their defeat at Bufhy-run, when they forfook all their remaining fettlements in this part of the country, as has been mentioned above.

ABOUT two miles before the army came to Beaver-creek, one of our people who had been made prifoner by fix Delawares about a week before, near Fort Bedford, having made his efcape from them, came and informed the Colonel that thefe Indians had

had the day before fallen in with the army, but kept themfelves concealed, being furprifed at our numbers. Two miles beyond Beaver-creek, by two fmall fprings, was feen the fcull of a child, that had been fixed on a pole by the Indians. The Tracts of 15 Indians were this day difcovered. The camp No. 5 is feven miles one quarter and fifty feven perches from big Beaver-creek; the whole march of this day being about twelve miles.

SUNDAY 7th October, paffing a high ridge, they had a fine profpect of an extenfive country to the right, which in general appeared level, with abundance of tall timber. The camp No. 6 lies at the foot of a fteep defcent, in a rich valley, on a ftrong ground, three fides thereof furrounded by a hollow, and on the fourth fide a fmall hill, which was occupied by a detached guard. This day's march was fix miles fixty five perches.

MONDAY 8th October, the army croffed little Beaver-creek, and one of its branches. This creek is eight perches wide, with a good ford, the country about it interfperfed with hills, rivulets and rich valleys, like that defcribed above. Camp No. 7 lies by a fmall run on the fide of a hill, commanding the

the ground about it, and is diftant eleven miles one quarter and forty nine perches from the laft encampment.

TUESDAY October 9th. In this day's march, the path divided into two branches, that to the fouthweft leading to the lower towns upon the Mufkingham. In the forks of the path ftand feveral trees painted by the Indians, in a hieroglyphic manner, denoting the number of wars in which they have been engaged, and the particulars of their fuccefs in prifoners and fcalps. The camp No. 8. lies on a run, and level piece of ground, with Yellow-creek clofe on the left, and a rifing ground near the rear of the right face. The path after the army left the forks was fo brufhy and entangled, that they were obliged to cut all the way before them, and alfo to lay feveral bridges, in order to make it paffable for the horfes; fo that this day they proceeded only five miles, three quarters and feventy perches.

WEDNESDAY 10th. Marched one mile with Yellow-creek on the left at a fmall diftance all the way, and croffed it at a good ford fifty feet wide; proceeding through an alternate fucceffion of fmall hills and rich vales, finely watered with
rivulets,

rivulets, to camp No. 9. feven miles and fixty perches in the whole.

THURSDAY 11th. Croffed a branch of Mufkingham river about fifty feet wide, the country much the fame as that defcribed above, difcovering a good deal of free-ftone. The camp No. 10. had this branch of the river parallel to its left face, and lies ten miles one quarter and forty perches from the former encampment.

FRIDAY 12th. Keeping the aforefaid creek on their left, they marched through much fine land, watered with fmall rivers and fprings; proceeding likewife through feveral favannahs or cleared fpots, which are by nature extremely beautiful; the fecond which they paffed being, in particular, one continued plain of near two miles, with a fine rifing ground forming a femicircle round the right hand fide, and a pleafant ftream of water at about a quarter of a mile diftant on the left. The camp No. 11. has the abovementioned branch of Mufkingham on the left, and is diftant ten miles and three quarters from the laft encampment.

SATURDAY 13th. Croffed Nemenfhehelas creek, about fifty feet wide, a little above where it empties
itfelf

itself into the aforesaid branch of Muskingham, having in their way a pleasant prospect over a large plain, for near two miles on the left. A little further, they came to another small river which they crossed about fifty perches above where it empties into the said branch of Muskingham. Here a high ridge on the right, and the creek close on the left, form a narrow defile about seventy perches long. Passing afterwards over a very rich bottom, they came to the main branch of Muskingham, about seventy yards wide, with a good ford. A little below and above the forks of this river is Tuscarowas, a place exceedingly beautiful by situation, the lands rich on both sides of the river; the country on the north-west side being an entire level plain, upwards of five miles in circumference. From the ruined houses appearing here, the Indians who inhabited the place and are now with the Delawares, are supposed to have had about one hundred and fifty warriors. This camp No. 12. is distant eight miles nineteen perches from the former.

SUNDAY 14th. The army remained in camp; and two men who had been dispatched by Colonel Bouquet from Fort-Pitt, with letters for Colonel Bradstreet, returned and reported—"That, within
"a few

"a few miles of this place, they had been made "prifoners by the Delawares, and carried to one "of their towns fixteen miles from hence, where "they were kept, till the favages, knowing of the "arrival of the army here, fet them at liberty, "ordering them to acquaint the Colonel that the "head men of the Delawares and Shawanefe were "coming as foon as poffible to treat of peace "with him."

MONDAY 15th. The army moved two miles forty perches further down the Mufkingham to camp No. 13, fituated on a very high bank, with the river at the foot of it, which is upwards of 100 yards wide at this place, with a fine level country at fome diftance from its banks, producing ftately timber, free from underwood, and plenty of food for cattle.

THE day following, fix Indians came to inform the Colonel that all their chiefs were affembled about eight miles from the camp, and were ready to treat with him of peace, which they were earn-eftly defirous of obtaining. He returned for anfwer that he would meet them the next day in a bower at fome diftance from the camp. In the mean time, he ordered a fmall ftockaded fort

to

to be built to depofite provifions for the ufe of the troops on their return; and to lighten the convoy.

As feveral large bodies of Indians were now within a few miles of the camp, whofe former inftances of treachery, although they now declared they came for peace, made it prudent to truft nothing to their intentions, the ftricteft orders were repeated to prevent a furprife.

WEDNESDAY 17th. The Colonel, with moft of the regular troops, Virginia volunteers and light horfe, marched from the camp to the bower erected for the congrefs. And foon after the troops were ftationed, fo as to appear to the beft advantage, the Indians arrived, and were conducted to the bower. Being feated, they began, in a fhort time, to fmoak their pipe or calumet, agreeable to their cuftom. This ceremony being over, their fpeakers laid down their pipes, and opened their pouches, wherein were their ftrings and belts of wampum. The Indians prefent were,

SENECAS.

Kiyafhuta, chief with 15 warriors.

DELAWARES.

DELAWARES.

Cuſtaloga, chief of the Wolfe-tribe, Beaver, chief of the Turky-tribe, with 20 warriors.

SHAWANESE.

Keiffinautchtha, a chief, and 6 warriors.

Kiyaſhuta, Turtle-Heart, Cuſtaloga and Beaver, were the ſpeakers.

THE general subſtance of what they had to offer, confiſted in excuſes for their late treachery and miſconduct, throwing the blame on the raſhneſs of their young men and the nations living to the weſtward of them, ſuing for peace in the moſt abject manner, and promiſing ſeverally to deliver up all their priſoners. After they had concluded, the Colonel promiſed to give them an anſwer the next day, and then diſmiſſed them, the army returning to the camp. — The badneſs of the weather, however, prevented his meeting them again till the 20th, when he ſpoke to them in ſubſtance as follows, viz.

"THAT their pretences to palliate their guilt
" by throwing the blame on the weſtern nations,
" and the raſhneſs of their young men, were weak
" and

"and frivolous, as it was in our power to have
"protected them againſt all theſe nations, if they
"had ſolicited our aſſiſtance, and that it was their
"own duty to have chaſtiſed their young men
"when they did wrong, and not to ſuffer them-
"ſelves to be directed by them."

He recapitulated to them many inſtances of their former perfidy—"their killing or captivat-
"ing the traders who had been ſent among them
"at their own requeſt, and plundering their effects;
"—their attacking Fort Pitt, which had been built
"with their expreſs conſent; their murdering four
"men that had been ſent on a public meſſage to
"them, thereby violating the cuſtoms held ſacred
"among all nations, however barbarous;——their
"attacking the King's troops laſt year in the woods,
"and after being defeated in that attempt, falling
"upon our frontiers, where they had continued to
"murder our people to this day, &c."——

He told them how treacherously they had violated even their late engagements with Colonel Bradſtreet, to whom they had promiſed to deliver up their priſoners by the 10th of September laſt, and to recall all their warriors from the frontiers, which they had been ſo far from complying with, that

that the prifoners ftill remained in their cuftody, and fome of their people were even now continuing their depredations; adding, that thefe things which he had mentioned, were only "a fmall part "of their numberlefs murders and breaches of "faith; and that their conduct had always been "equally perfidious.——You have, faid he, prom-
"ifed at every former treaty, as you do now, that "you would deliver up all your prifoners, and "have received every time, on that account, "confiderable prefents, but have never complied "with that or any other engagement. I am now "to tell you, therefore, that we will be no longer "impofed upon by your promifes. This army "fhall not leave your country till you have fully "complied with every condition that is to precede "my treaty with you.

"I HAVE brought with me the relations of the "people you have maffacred, or taken prifoners. "They are impatient for revenge; and it is with "great difficulty that I can protect you againft "their juft refentment, which is only reftrained by "the affurances given them that no peace fhall "ever be concluded till ycu have given us full "fatisfaction." —

"YOUR

"Your former allies, the Ottawas, Chipwas,
"Wyandots, and others, have made their peace
"with us. The Six Nations have joined us againſt
"you. We now ſurround you, having poſſeſſion
"of all the waters of the Ohio, the Miſſiſippi, the
"Miamis, and the lakes. All the French living
"in thoſe parts are now ſubjects of Great-Britain,
"and dare no longer aſſiſt you. It is therefore in
"our power totally to extirpate you from being a
"people —— But the Engliſh are a merciful and
"generous nation, averſe to ſhed the blood, even
"of their moſt cruel enemies; and if it was poſſi-
"ble that you could convince us, that you ſincerely
"repent of your paſt perfidy, and that we could
"depend on your good behavior for the future,
"you might yet hope for mercy and peace —— If
"I find that you faithfully execute the following
"preliminary conditions, I will not treat you with
"the ſeverity you deſerve.

"I give you twelve days from this date to
"deliver into my hands at Wakatamake all the
"priſoners in your poſſeſſion, without any ex-
"ception; Engliſhmen, Frenchmen, women and
"children; whether adopted in your tribes, mar-
"ried, or living amongſt you under any denomi-
"nation and pretence whatſoever, together with
"all

"all negroes. And you are to furnish the said "prisoners with cloathing, provisions, and horses, "to carry them to Fort Pitt.

"WHEN you have fully complied with these "conditions, you shall then know on what terms "you may obtain the peace you sue for."—

THIS speech made an impression on the minds of the savages, which, it is hoped, will not soon be eradicated. The firm and determined spirit with which the Colonel delivered himself, their consciousness of the aggravated injuries they had done us, and the view of the same commander and army that had so severely chastised them at Bushy-Run the preceding year, now advanced into the very heart of their remote settlements, after penetrating through wildernesses which they had deemed impassable by regular troops —— all these things contributed to bend the haughty temper of the savages to the lowest degree of abasement; so that even their speeches seem to exhibit but few specimens of that strong and ferocious eloquence, which their inflexible spirit of independency has on former occasions inspired. And though it is not to be doubted, if an opportunity had offered, but they would have fallen upon our army with their

usual

usual fierceness, yet when they saw the vigilance and spirit of our troops were such, that they could neither be attacked nor surprized with any prospect of success, their spirits seemed to revolt from the one extreme of insolent boldness, to the other of abject timidity. And happy will it be for them and for us, if the instances of our humanity and mercy, which they experienced in that critical situation, shall make as lasting impressions on their savage dispositions, as it is believed the instances of our bravery and power have done; so that they may come to unite, with their fear of the latter, a love of the former; and have their minds gradually opened, by such examples, to the mild dictates of peace and civility.

The reader, it is to be hoped, will readily excuse this digression, if it should be thought one. I now resume our narrative. The two Delaware chiefs, at the close of their speech on the 17th, delivered eighteen white prisoners, and eighty-three small sticks, expressing the number of other prisoners which they had in their possession, and promised to bring in as soon as possible. None of the Shawanese Kings appeared at the congress, and Keissinautchtha their deputy declined speaking until the Colonel had answered the Delawares, and then

then with a dejected fullennefs he promifed, in behalf of his nation, that they would fubmit to the terms prefcribed to the other tribes.

THE Colonel however, determined to march farther into their country, knowing that the prefence of his army would be the beft fecurity for the performance of their promifes; and required fome of each nation to attend him in his march.

KIYASHUTA addreffed the feveral nations, before their departure, "defiring them to be ftrong in "complying with their engagements, that they "might wipe away the reproach of their former "breach of faith, and convince their brothers the "Englifh that they could fpeak the truth; adding "that he would conduct the army to the place "appointed for receiving the prifoners."

MONDAY October 22d. The army, attended by the Indian deputies, marched nine miles to camp No. 14. croffing Margaret's creek about fifty feet wide —— The day following, they proceeded fixteen miles one quarter and feventy feven perches farther to camp No. 15. and halted there one day.

THURSDAY

THURSDAY 25. They marched six miles, one half and sixteen perches to camp No. 16, situated within a mile of the Forks of Muskingham; and this place was fixed upon instead of Wakautamike, as the most central and convenient place to receive the prisoners; for the principal Indian towns now lay around them, distant from seven to twenty miles; excepting only the lower Shawanese town situated on Scioto river, which was about eighty miles; so that from this place the army had it in their power to awe all the enemy's settlements and destroy their towns, if they should not punctually fulfil the engagements they had entered into.—— Four redoubts were built here opposite to the four angles of the camp; the ground in the front was cleared, a store-house for the provisions erected, and likewise a house to receive, and treat of peace with, the Indians, when they should return. Three houses with separate apartments were also raised for the reception of the captives of the respective provinces, and proper officers appointed to take charge of them, with a matron to attend the women and children; so that with the officers mess houses, ovens, &c. this camp had the appearance of a little town in which the greatest order and regularity were observed.

ON

On Saturday 27th. A meffenger arrived from king Cuftaloga, informing that he was on his way with his prifoners, and alfo a meffenger from the lower Shawanefe towns of the like import. The Colonel however, having no reafon to fufpect the latter nation of backwardnefs, fent one of their own people, defiring them — "to be punctual as "to the time fixed; to provide a fufficient quantity "of provifions to fubfift the prifoners; to bring "the letters wrote to him laft winter by the French "commandant at Fort Chartres, which fome of "their people had ftopped ever fince;" adding that, "as their nation had expreffed fome un- "eafinefs at our not fhaking hands with them, "they were to know that the Englifh never took "their enemies by the hand, before peace was "finally concluded."

The day following, the Shawanefe meffenger returned, faying that when he had proceeded as far as Wakautamike, the chief of that town undertook to proceed with the meffage himfelf, and defired the other to return and acquaint the Englifh that all his prifoners were ready, and he was going to the lower towns to haften theirs.

OCTOBER 28th. Peter the Caughnawaga chief, and twenty Indians of that nation arrived from Sandufki, with a letter from Colonel Bradftreet, in anfwer to one which Colonel Bouquet had fent to him from Fort-Pitt, by two of the Indians who firft fpoke to him in favour of the Shawanefe, as hath been already mentioned. The fubftance of Colonel Bradftreet's letter was "that he had fettled "nothing with the Shawanefe and Delawares, nor "received any prifoners from them.—That he "had acquainted all the Indian nations, as far as "the Ilinois, the bay, &c. with the inftructions "he had received from General Gage, refpecting "the peace he had lately made; that he had been "in Sandufki-lake and up the river, as far as "navigable for Indian canoes, for near a month; "but that he found it impoffible to ftay longer in "thefe parts; abfolute neceffity obliging him to "turn off the other way," &c.

COLONEL BRADSTREET, without doubt, did all which circumftances would permit, in his department; but his not being able to remain at Sandufki agreeable to the original plan, till matters were finally fettled with the Ohio Indians, would have been an unfavourable incident, if Colonel Bouquet had not now had the chiefs of fundry tribes

Colonel Bouquet's Expedition. 63

tribes with him, and was fo far advanced into the Indian country, that they thought it advifeable to fubmit to the conditions impofed upon them.

THE Caughnawagas reported that the Indians on the lakes had delivered but few of their prifoners; that the Ottawas had killed a great part of theirs, and the other nations had either done the fame, or elfe kept them.

FROM this time to November 9th, was chiefly fpent in fending and receiving meffages to and from the Indian towns, relative to the prifoners, who were now coming into the camp one day after another in fmall parties, as the different nations arrived in whofe poffeffion they had been. The Colonel kept fo ftedfaftly to this article of having every prifoner delivered, that when the Delaware kings, Beaver and Cuftaloga, had brought in all theirs except twelve, which they promifed to bring in a few days, he refufed to fhake hands or have the leaft talk with them, while a fingle captive remained among them.

BY the 9th of November, moft of the prifoners were arrived that could be expected this feafon,
amounting

amounting to 206 * in the whole; befides about 100 more in poffeffion of the Shawanefe, which they promifed to deliver the following fpring. Mr. Smallman, formerly a major in the Pennfylvania troops, who had been taken laft fummer near Detroit by the Wyandots, and delivered to the Shawanefe, was among the number of thofe whom they now brought in, and informed the Colonel that the reafon of their not bringing the remainder of their prifoners, was that many of their principal men, to whom they belonged, were gone to trade with the French, and would not return for fix weeks; but that every one of their nation who were at home, had either brought or fent theirs. He further faid that, on the army's firft coming into the country, it had been reported among the Shawanefe that our intention was to deftroy them all, on which they had refolved to kill their prifoners and fight us; that a French trader who was with them, and had many barrels of powder and ball, made them a prefent of the

---

* Virginians	Males,	32
	Females and Children,	58
Pennfylvanians,	Males,	49
	Females and Children,	67
	In all	206

whole,

whole, as foon as they had come to this refolution; but that, happily for the poor captives, juft as the Shawanefe were preparing to execute this tragedy, they received the Colonel's meffage, informing them that his intentions were only to receive the prifoners and to make peace with them on the fame terms he fhould give to the Delawares.

ON this intelligence they fufpended their cruel purpofe, and began to collect as many of the prifoners as they had power to deliver; but hearing immediately afterwards that one of our foldiers had been killed near the camp at Mufkingham, and that fome of their nation were fufpected as guilty of the murder, they again imagined they would fall under our refentment, and therefore determined once more to ftand out againft us. For which purpofe, after having brought their prifoners as far as Wakautamike, where they heard this news, they collected them all into a field and were going to kill them, when a fecond exprefs providentially arrived from Colonel Bouquet, who affured them that their nation was not even fufpected of having any concern in the aforefaid murder; upon which they proceeded to the camp to deliver up the captives, who had thus twice fo narrowly efcaped becoming the victims of their barbarity.

ON

On Friday, November 9th, the Colonel, attended by moſt of the principal officers, went to the conference-houſe. The Senecas and Delawares were firſt treated with. Kiyaſhuta and ten warriors repreſented the former. Cuſtaloga and twenty warriors the latter.

Kiyashuta ſpoke —— "With this ſtring of "wampum, we wipe the tears from your eyes — "we deliver you theſe three priſoners, which are the "laſt of your fleſh and blood that remained among "the Senecas and Cuſtaloga's tribe of Delawares, "we gather together and bury with this belt† all "the bones of the people that have been killed "during this unhappy war, which the Evil Spirit "occaſioned among us. We cover the bones that "have been buried, that they may never more be "remembered — We again cover their place with "leaves that it may be no more ſeen. — As we "have been long aſtray, and the path between "you and us ſtopped, we extend this belt that it "may be again cleared, and we may travel in "peace to ſee our brethren as our anceſtors for-"merly did. While you hold it faſt by one end, "and we by the other, we ſhall always be able to

† A belt or ſtring is always delivered when thus mentioned.

"diſcover

"discover any thing that may disturb our friend-
"ship."—

THE Colonel answered that "he had heard them
"with pleasure; that he received these three last
"prisoners they had to deliver, and joined in
"burying the bones of those who had fallen in
"the war, so that their place might be no more
"known. The peace you ask for, you shall now
"have. The king, my master and your father,
"has appointed me only to make war; but he has
"other servants who are employed in the work of
"peace. Sir William Johnson is empowered for
"that purpose. To him you are to apply; but
"before I give you leave to go, two things are to
"be settled.

1. "As peace cannot be finally concluded here,
"you will deliver me two hostages for the Senecas,
"and two for Custaloga's tribe, to remain in our
"hands at Fort Pitt, as a security, that you shall
"commit no further hostilities or violence against
"any of his majesty's subjects; and when the
"peace is concluded these hostages shall be deliv-
"ered safe back to you.

2. "THE deputies you are to send to Sir William
"Johnson,

"Johnson, must be fully empowered to treat for
"your tribes, and you shall engage to abide by
"whatever they stipulate. In that treaty, every
"thing concerning trade and other matters will be
"settled by Sir William, to render the peace ever-
"lasting; and the deputies you are to send to him,
"as well as the hostages to be delivered to me,
"are to be named and presented to me for my
"approbation." ——

The Colonel, after promising to deliver back two of their people, Capt. Pipe, and Capt. John, whom he had detained at Fort-Pitt, took the chiefs by the hand for the first time, which gave them great joy.

THE next conference was on November 10th, with the Turky and Turtle tribes of Delawares, King Beaver their chief and thirty warriors representing the former; and Kelappama brother to their chief * with twenty-five warriors the latter. The Senecas and Custaloga's tribe of Delawares were also present. Their speech and the answer given, were much the same as above; excepting

---

* The Chief of the Turtle-tribe, for some reason, chose to absent himself.

that

that the Colonel infifted on their delivering up an Englifhman, who had murdered one of our people on the frontiers and brought the fcalp to them; and that they fhould appoint the fame number of deputies and deliver the fame number of hoftages, for each of their tribes, as had been ftipulated for Cuftaloga's tribe.

NOVEMBER 11. King Beaver prefented fix hoftages to remain with Col. Bouquet, and five deputies to treat with Sir William Johnfon, who were approved of. This day he acquainted the chiefs prefent that as he had great reafon to be diffatisfied with the conduct of Nettowhatways, the chief of the Turtle tribe who had not appeared, he therefore depofed him; and that tribe were to chufe and prefent another for his approbation. This they did a few days afterwards — Smile not, reader, at this tranfaction; for though it may not be attended with fo many fplendid and flattering circumftances to a commander, as the depofing an Eaft Indian Nabob or chief; yet to penetrate into the wildernefles where thofe ftern Weft Indian Chieftains hold their fway, and to frown them from their throne; though but compofed of the unhewn log, will be found to require both refolution and firmnefs; and their fubmitting

to

to it clearly shews to what degree of humiliation they were reduced.

But to proceed. The Shawanese still remained to be treated with, and though this nation saw themselves under the necessity of yielding to the same conditions with the other tribes, yet there had appeared a dilatoriness and sullen haughtiness in all their conduct, which rendered it very suspicious.

The 12th of November was appointed for the conference with them; which was managed on their part by Keissinautchtha and Nimwha their chiefs, with the Red Hawke, Lavissimo, Bensivasica, Eweecunwee, Keigleighque, and forty warriors; the Caughnawaga, Seneca and Delaware chiefs, with about sixty warriors, being also present.

The Red Hawke was their speaker, and as he delivered himself with a strange mixture of fierce pride, and humble submission, I shall add a passage or two from his speech.

"Brother,

"You will listen to us your younger brothers;
"and as we discover something in your eyes that
"looks dissatisfaction with us, we now wipe away
"every

"every thing bad between us that you may clearly
"fee—You have heard many bad ſtories of us—
"We clean your ears that you may hear—We
"remove every thing bad from your heart, that
"it may be like the heart of your anceſtors, when
"they thought of nothing but good." [Here he
gave a ſtring.]

"BROTHER; when we ſaw you coming this road,
"you advanced towards us with a tomahawk in
"your hand; but we your younger brothers take it
"out of your hands and throw it up to God † to
"diſpoſe of as he pleaſes; by which means we
"hope never to ſee it more. And now, brother,
"we beg leave that you who are a warrior, will
"take hold of this chain (giving a ſtring) of
"friendſhip, and receive it from us, who are alſo
"warriors, and let us think no more of war, in
"pity to our old men, women and children"—
Intimating, by this laſt expreſſion, that it was
mere compaſſion to them, and not inability to
fight, that made their nation defire peace.

† Their uſual figure for making peace is burying the hatchet;
but as ſuch hatchets may be dug up again, perhaps he thought this
new expreſſion of "ſending it up to God, or the Good Spirit,"
a much ſtronger emblem of the permanency and ſtedfaſtneſs of
the peace now to be made.

HE

He then produced a treaty held with the government of Pennsylvania 1701, and three meſſages or letters from that government of different dates; and concluded thus —

"Now, Brother, I beg We who are warriors
"may forget our diſputes, and renew the friend-
"ſhip which appears by theſe papers to have ſub-
"ſiſted between our fathers." — He promiſed, in behalf of the reſt of their nation, who were gone to a great diſtance to hunt, and could not have notice to attend the treaty, that they ſhould certainly come to Fort-Pitt in the ſpring, and bring the remainder of the priſoners with them.

As the ſeaſon was far advanced, and the Colonel could not ſtay long in theſe remote parts, he was obliged to reſt ſatisfied with the priſoners the Shawaneſe had brought; taking hoſtages, and laying them under the ſtrongeſt obligations, for the delivery of the reſt; knowing that no other effectual method could at preſent be purſued.

He expoſtulated with them on account of their paſt conduct, and told them — "that the ſpeech "they had delivered would have been agreeable to "him, if their actions had correſponded with their "words.

"words. You have fpoken, faid he, much of
"peace, but have neglected to comply with the
"only condition, upon which you can obtain it.
"Keiffinautchtha, one of your chiefs, met me a
"month ago at Tufcarawas, and accepted the fame
"terms of peace for your nation, that were pre-
"fcribed to the Senecas and Delawares; promifing
"in ten days from that time to meet me here with
"all your prifoners — After waiting for you till
"now, you are come at laft, only with a part of
"them, and propofe putting off the delivery of
"the reft till the fpring. — What right have you
"to expect different terms from thofe granted to
"the Delawares, &c. who have given me entire
"fatisfaction by their ready fubmiffion to every
"thing required of them? —— But I will cut this
"matter fhort with you; and before I explain
"myfelf further, I infift on your immediate anfwer
"to the following queftions —

1ft. "Will you forthwith collect and deliver up
"all the prifoners yet in your poffeffion, and the
"French living among you, with all the Negroes
"you have taken from us in this or any other
"war; and that without any exception or evafion
"whatfoever?"

2d. "WILL

2d. "WILL you deliver fix hoftages into my
"hands as a fecurity for your punctual perform-
"ance of the above article, and that your nations
"fhall commit no farther hoftilities againft the
"perfons or property of his majefty's fubjects?"

BENEVISSICO replied that "they agreed to give
"the hoftages required, and faid that he himfelf
"would immediately return to their lower towns
"and collect all our flefh and blood that remained
"among them, and that we fhould fee them at
"Fort-Pitt † as foon as poffible.—That, as to the
"French, they had no power over them. They
"were fubjects to the king of England. We
"might do with them what we pleafed; though
"he believed they were all returned before this
"time to their own country."—

THEY then delivered their hoftages, and the
Colonel told them "that though he had brought
"a Tomahawk in his hand, yet as they had now
"fubmitted, he would not let it fall on their heads,
"but let it drop to the ground, no more to be
"feen. He exhorted them to exercife kindnefs to

---

† It will appear, by the poftfcript to this account, that the
Shawanefe have fulfilled this engagement.

"the

"the captives, and look upon them now as brothers
"and no longer prifoners; adding, that he intended
"to fend fome of their relations along with the
"Indians, to fee their friends collected and brought
"to Fort-Pitt. He promifed to give them letters
"to Sir William Johnfon, to facilitate a final
"peace, and defired them to be ftrong in perform-
"ing every thing ftipulated."

THE Caughnawagas, the Delawares and Senecas, feverally addreffed the Shawanefe, as grandchildren and nephews, "to perform their promifes, and to "be ftrong in doing good, that this peace might "be everlafting."—

AND here I am to enter on a fcene, referved on purpofe for this place, that the thread of the foregoing narrative might not be interrupted—a fcene, which language indeed can but weakly defcribe; and to which the Poet or Painter might have repaired to enrich their higheft colourings of the variety of human paffions; the Philofopher to find ample fubject for his moft ferious reflections; and the Man to exercife all the tender and fympathetic feelings of the foul.

THE fcene I mean, was the arrival of the
prifoners

prisoners in the camp; where were to be seen fathers and mothers recognizing and clasping their once-lost babes; husbands hanging round the necks of their newly-recovered wives; sisters and brothers unexpectedly meeting together after long separation, scarce able to speak the same language, or, for some time, to be sure that they were children of the same parents! In all these interviews, joy and rapture inexpressible were seen, while feelings of a very different nature were painted in the looks of others; — flying from place to place in eager enquiries after relatives not found! trembling to receive an answer to their questions! distracted with doubts, hopes and fears, on obtaining no account of those they sought for! or stiffened into living monuments of horror and woe, on learning their unhappy fate!

THE Indians too, as if wholly forgetting their usual savageness, bore a capital part in heightening this most affecting scene. They delivered up their beloved captives with the utmost reluctance; shed torrents of tears over them, recommending them to the care and protection of the commanding officer. Their regard to them continued all the time they remained in camp. They visited them from day to day; and brought them what corn,
skins,

skins, horses and other matters, they had bestowed on them, while in their families; accompanied with other presents, and all the marks of the most sincere and tender affection. Nay, they did not stop here, but, when the army marched, some of the Indians solicited and obtained leave to accompany their former captives all the way to Fort-Pitt, and employed themselves in hunting and bringing provisions for them on the road. A young Mingo carried this still further, and gave an instance of love which would make a figure even in romance. A young woman of Virginia was among the captives, to whom he had formed so strong an attachment, as to call her his wife. Against all remonstrances of the imminent danger to which he exposed himself by approaching to the frontiers, he persisted in following her, at the risk of being killed by the surviving relations of many unfortunate persons, who had been captivated or scalped by those of his nation.

THOSE qualities in savages challenge our just esteem. They should make us charitably consider their barbarities as the effects of wrong education, and false notions of bravery and heroism; while we should look on their virtues as sure marks that nature has made them fit subjects of cultivation as well as us; and that we are called by our superior advantages to yield them all the helps we can in this way. Cruel and unmerciful as they are, by habit and long example, in war, yet whenever they come to give way to the native dictates of humanity, they exercife virtues which Chriftians need not blufh to imitate. When they once determine to give life, they give every thing with it, which, in their apprehenfion, belongs to it. From every enquiry that has been made, it appears — that no woman thus faved is preferved from bafe motives, or need fear the violation of her honour. No child is otherwife treated by the perfons adopting it than the children of their own body. The perpetual flavery of thofe captivated in war, is a notion which even their barbarity has not yet fuggefted to them. Every captive whom their affection, their caprice, or whatever elfe, leads them to fave, is foon incorporated with them, and fares alike with themfelves.

These inftances of Indian tendernefs and humanity were thought worthy of particular notice. The like inftances among our own people will not feem ftrange; and therefore I fhall only mention one, out of a multitude that might be given on this occafion.

AMONG

The Indians delivering up the English Captives to Colonel Bouquet near his Camp at the Forks of Muskingum in North America in Nov.r 1764.

AMONG the captives, a woman was brought into the camp at Mufkingham, with a babe about three months old at her breaft. One of the Virginia-volunteers foon knew her to be his wife, who had been taken by the Indians about fix months before. She was immediately delivered to her overjoyed hufband. He flew with her to his tent, and cloathed her and his child in proper apparel. But their joy, after the firft tranfports, was foon damped by the reflection that another dear child of about two years old, captivated with the mother, and feparated from her, was ftill miffing, altho' many children had been brought in.

A FEW days afterwards, a number of other prifoners were brought to the camp, among whom were feveral more children. The woman was fent for, and one, fuppofed to be hers, was produced to her. At firft fight fhe was uncertain, but viewing the child with great earneftnefs, fhe foon recollected its features; and was fo overcome with joy, that literally forgetting her fucking child fhe dropt it from her arms, and catching up the new found child in an extafy, preffed it to her breaft, and burfting into tears carried it off, unable to fpeak for joy. The father feizing up the babe fhe had let fall, followed her in no lefs tranfport and affection.

AMONG

Among the children who had been carried off young, and had long lived with the Indians, it is not to be expected that any marks of joy would appear on being restored to their parents or relatives. Having been accustomed to look upon the Indians as the only connexions they had, having been tenderly treated by them, and speaking their language, it is no wonder that they considered their new state in the light of a captivity, and parted from the savages with tears.

But it must not be denied that there were even some grown persons who shewed an unwillingness to return. The Shawanese were obliged to bind several of their prisoners and force them along to the camp; and some women, who had been delivered up, afterwards found means to escape and run back to the Indian towns. Some, who could not make their escape, clung to their savage acquaintance at parting, and continued many days in bitter lamentations, even refusing sustenance.

For the honour of humanity, we would suppose those persons to have been of the lowest rank, either bred up in ignorance and distressing penury, or who had lived so long with the Indians as to forget all their former connections. For, easy and unconstrained unconftrained as the favage life is, certainly it could never be put in competition with the bleffings of improved life and the light of religion, by any perfons who have had the happinefs of enjoying, and the capacity of difcerning, them.

EVERY thing being now fettled with the Indians, the army decamped on Sunday 18th November, and marched for Fort-Pitt, where it arrived on the 28th. The regular troops were immediately fent to garrifon the different pofts on the communication, and the provincial troops, with the captives, to their feveral provinces. Here ended this expedition, in which it is remarkable that, notwithftanding the many difficulties attending it, the troops were never in want of any neceffaries; continuing perfectly healthy during the whole campaign; in which no life was loft, except the man mentioned to have been killed at Mufkingham.

In the beginning of January 1765, Colonel Bouquet arrived at Philadelphia, receiving, whereever he came, every poffible mark of gratitude and efteem from the people in general; and particularly from the overjoyed relations of the captives, whom he had fo happily, and without bloodfhed, reftored to their country and friends. Nor was
the

the legiflative part of the provinces lefs fenfible of his important fervices. The affembly of Pennfylvania, at their firft fitting, unanimoufly voted him the following addrefs.

In ASSEMBLY, January 15, 1765, A. M.

To the Honourable HENRY BOUQUET, Efq;

Commander in Chief of His MAJESTY's Forces in the Southern Department of AMERICA,

The Addrefs of the Reprefentatives of the Freemen of the Province of Pennfylvania, in General Affembly met.

SIR,

'THE reprefentatives of the freemen of the
' province of Pennfylvania, in general affem-
' bly met, being informed that you intend fhortly
' to embark for England, and moved with a due
' fenfe of the important fervices you have rendered
' to his majefty, his northern colonies in general,
' and to this province in particular, during our
' late wars with the French and barbarous Indians,
' in the remarkable victory over the favage enemy,
' united to oppofe you, near Bufhy-Run, in Auguft
' 1763,

'1763, when on your march for the relief of Pitts-
'burg, owing, under God, to your intrepidity
'and fuperior fkill in command, together with the
'bravery of your officers and little army; as alfo
'in your late march to the country of the favage
'nations, with the troops under your direction;
'thereby ftriking terror through the numerous
'Indian tribes around you; laying a foundation
'for a lafting as well as honourable peace with
'them; and refcuing, from favage captivity, up-
'wards of two hundred of our chriftian brethren,
'prifoners among them: thefe eminent fervices,
'and your conftant attention to the civil rights of
'his majefty's fubjects in this province, demand,
'Sir, the grateful tribute of thanks from all good
'men; and therefore we, the reprefentatives of the
'freemen of Pennfylvania, unanimoufly for our-
'felves, and in behalf of all the people of this
'province, do return you our moft fincere and
'hearty thanks for thefe your great fervices, wifh-
'ing you a fafe and pleafant voyage to England,
'with a kind and gracious reception from his
'majefty.
  'Signed, by order of the Houfe,
    'JOSEPH FOX, Speaker.'

The

The Colonel's Anfwer was as follows, viz.

To the Honourable the Representatives of the Freemen of the province of Pennfylvania, in General Affembly met.

'Gentlemen,

'WITH a heart impreffed with the moft
' lively fenfe of gratitude, I return you my
' humble and fincere thanks, for the honour you
' have done me in your polite addrefs of the 15th
' of January, tranfmitted me to New-York by
' your fpeaker.

'Next to the approbation of His Sacred Maj-
' efty, and my fuperiour officers, nothing could
' afford me higher pleafure than your favour-
' able opinion of my conduct, in the difcharge of
' thofe military commands with which I have been
' intrufted.

'Gratitude as well as juftice demand of me
' to acknowlege, that the aids granted by the leg-
' iflature of this province, and the conftant affift-
' ance and fupport afforded me by the honourable
' the Governor and Commiffioners in the late
' expedition, have enabled me to recover fo many
' of his Majefty's fubjects from a cruel captivity,
'and

'and be the happy inftrument of reftoring them
'to freedom and liberty: To you therefore, gen-
'tlemen, is the greater fhare of that merit due,
'which you are generoufly pleafed on this occafion
'to impute to my fervices.

'YOUR kind teftimony of my conftant attention
'to the civil rights of his majefty's fubjects in this
'Province, does me fingular honour, and calls for
'the return of my warmeft acknowledgments.

'PERMIT me to take this public opportunity of
'doing juftice to the officers of the regular and
'provincial troops, and the volunteers, who have
'ferved with me, by declaring that, under Divine
'Providence, the repeated fucceffes of his Majefty's
'arms againft a favage enemy, are principally to be
'afcribed to their courage and refolution, and to
'their perfeverance under the fevereft hardfhips
'and fatigue.

'I SINCERELY wifh profperity and happinefs to
'the province, and have the honour to be, with
'the greateft refpect, Gentlemen,
  'Your moft obedient, and moft humble fervant,
            'HENRY BOUQUET.'
February 4, 1765.

SOON

Soon afterwards the Colonel received a very polite and affectionate letter from Governor Fauquier, dated 25th of December, inclosing resolves of the honourable members of his Majesty's Council, and of the house of Burgesses, for the colony and dominion of Virginia.

Those respectable bodies unanimously returned their thanks to him for the activity, spirit and zeal, with which he had reduced the Indians to terms of peace, and compelled those savages to deliver up so many of his Majesty's subjects whom they had in captivity. They further requested the Governor to recommend him to his Majesty's ministers, as an officer of distinguished merit, in this and every former service in which he has been engaged.

The Colonel, in his answer, acknowledged the ready assistance and countenance which he had always received from the Governor and colony of Virginia in carrying on the King's service; and mentioned his particular obligations to Col. Lewis, for his zeal and good conduct during the campaign.

The honours thus bestowed on him, his own modesty

modefty made him defirous of transferring to the officers and army under his command; and indeed the mutual confidence and harmony fubfifting between him and them, highly redound to the reputation of both. He has taken every occafion of doing juftice to the particular merit of Colonel REID who was fecond in command; and alfo to all the officers who ferved in the expedition, regulars as well as provincials †.

THE reader will obferve that the public bodies who prefented thefe addreffes to the Colonel, not only wifhed to exprefs their own gratitude, but likewife to be inftrumental in recommending him to the advancement his fervices merited. And furely it is a happy circumftance to obtain promotion, not only unenvied, but even with the general approbation and good wifhes, of the public. It ought, however, to be mentioned, that on the firft account his Majefty received of this expedition, and long before thofe teftimonies could reach England, he was gracioufly pleafed of his own royal goodnefs and as a reward of the Colonel's merit, to promote him to the rank of BRIGADIER GEN-

---

† The Pennfylvania troops were commanded by Lieutenant Colonel Francis, and Lieutenant Colonel Clayton.

ERAL

ERAL, and to the command of the fouthern diftrict of America. And as he is rendered as dear, by his private virtues, to thofe who have the honour of his more intimate acquaintance, as he is by his military fervices to the public, it is hoped he may long continue among us; where his experienced abilities will enable him, and his love of the Englifh conftitution entitle him, to fill any future truft to which his Majefty may be pleafed to call him.———

POSTSCRIPT.

IT was mentioned in the 72d page of this account, that the Shawanefe brought only a part of their prifoners with them to Col. Bouquet at Mufkingham, in November laft; and that, as the feafon was far advanced, he was obliged to reft fatisfied with taking hoftages for the delivery of the remainder at Fort-Pitt, in the enfuing fpring.

THE efcape of thofe hoftages foon afterwards, as well as the former equivocal conduct of their nation, had given reafon to doubt the fincerity of their intentions with refpect to the performance of of their promifes. But we have the fatisfaction to find that they punctually have fulfilled them. Ten of their chiefs, and about fifty of their warriors, attended with many of their women and children, met GEORGE CROGHAN, Efq; deputy agent to Sir WILLIAM JOHNSON, at Fort-Pitt, the 9th of laft May; together with a large body of Delawares, Senecas, Sandufky and Munfy Indians; where they delivered the remainder of their prifoners, brightened the chain of friendfhip, and gave every affurance of their firm intentions to preferve the peace inviolable for ever.

THERE is fomething remarkable in the appellation they gave to the Englifh on this occafion; calling them Fathers inftead of Brethren.

LAWAUGHQUA, the Shawanefe fpeaker, delivered himfelf in the following terms. ——

"FATHERS, for fo we will call you henceforward;
" liften to what we are going to fay to you.

" IT gave us great pleafure yefterday to be called
" the children of the great King of England; and
" convinces us your intentions towards us are
" upright, as we know a Father will be tender of
" his

"his children, and they are more ready to obey
"him than a Brother. Therefore we hope our
"Father will now take better care of his children,
"than has heretofore been done.——

"You put us in mind of our promife to Col.
"Bouquet; which was to bring your flefh and
"blood to be delivered at this place. FATHER,
"you have not fpoke in vain—you fee we have
"brought them with us,—except a few that were
"out with our hunting parties, which will be
"brought here as foon as they return.

"THEY have been all united to us by adoption;
"and altho' we now deliver them up to you, we
"will always look upon them as our relations,
"whenever the Great Spirit is pleafed that we may
"vifit them.

"FATHER, We have taken as much care of them,
"as if they were our own flefh and blood. They
"are now become unacquainted with your cuftoms
"and manners; and therefore, we requeft you will
"ufe them tenderly and kindly, which will induce
"them to live contentedly with you.

"HERE is a belt with the figure of our Father
"the

"the King of Great-Britain at one end, and the "Chief of our nation at the other. It reprefents "them holding the chain of friendfhip; and we "hope neither fide will flip their hands from it, fo "long as the Sun and Moon give light."

THE reader will further remember that one of the engagements which the different Indian Tribes entered into with Colonel Bouquet, was to fend deputies to conclude a peace with Sir WILLIAM JOHNSON. This has alfo been punctually fulfilled; and we are affured that Sir WILLIAM "has finifhed "his congrefs greatly to his fatisfaction, and even "beyond his expectations." Thus every good confequence has enfued from this important expedition, which our fondeft wifhes could have induced us to expect from the known valour and fpirit of the able commander who had the conduct of it; and we now have the pleafure once more to behold the temple of JANUS fhut, in this weftern world!

REFLECTIONS

ON THE

WAR WITH THE SAVAGES OF NORTH-AMERICA.

THE long continued ravages of the Indians on the frontiers of the British colonies in America, and the fatal overthrows which they have sometimes given our best disciplined troops, especially in the beginning of the late war, have rendered them an object of our consideration, even in their military capacity. And as but few officers, who may be employed against them, can have opportunities to observe the true causes of their advantages over European troops in the woods, it is with the utmost pleasure that I now proceed to lay before the public the following valuable papers, which I mentioned† to have been communicated

† See the introduction.

to me by an officer of great abilities and long experience, in our wars with the Indians.

As scarce any thing has yet been published on a subject now become of the highest importance § to our colonies, these papers will undoubtedly be an acceptable present to the reader, and the remarks contained in them may be more and more improved by the future care and attention of able men, till perhaps a compleat system is at length formed for the conduct of this particular species of war.

---

§ It will appear by the account of Indian tribes and towns annexed to these papers, that the enemies we have to deal with are neither contemptible in numbers or strength.

SECTION I.

OF THE TEMPER AND GENIUS OF THE INDIANS.

THE love of liberty is innate in the favage; and feems the ruling paffion of the ftate of nature. His defires and wants, being few, are eafily gratified, and leave him much time to fpare, which he would fpend in idlenefs, if hunger did not force him to hunt. That exercife makes him ftrong, active and bold, raifes his courage, and fits him for war, in which he ufes the fame ftratagems and cruelty as againft the wild beafts; making no fcruple to employ treachery and perfidy to vanquifh his enemy.

JEALOUS of his independency and of his property, he will not fuffer the leaft encroachment on either; and upon the flighteft fufpicion, fired with refentment, he becomes an implacable enemy, and flies to arms to vindicate his right, or revenge an injury.

THE

The advantages of these savages over civilized nations are both natural and acquired. They are tall and well limbed, remarkable for their activity, and have a piercing eye and quick ear, which are of great service to them in the woods.

Like beasts of prey, they are patient, deceitful, and rendered by habit almost insensible to the common feelings of humanity. Their barbarous custom of scalping their enemies, in the heat of action; the exquisite torments often inflicted by them on those reserved for a more deliberate fate; their general ferocity of manners, and the successes wherewith they have often been flushed, have conspired to render their name terrible, and sometimes to strike a pannic even into our bravest and best disciplined troops.

Their acquired advantages are, that they have been inured to bear the extremes of heat and cold; and from their infancy, in winter and summer, to plunge themselves in cold streams, and to go almost naked, exposed to the scorching sun or nipping frosts, till they arrive to the state of manhood. Some of them destroy the sensation of the skin by scratching it with the short and sharp teeth of some animal, disposed in the form of a curry-comb, which

which makes them regardlefs of briars and thorns in running thro' thickets. Rivers are no obftacles to them in their wild excurfions. They either fwim over, or crofs them on rafts or canoes, of an eafy and ready conftruction.

In their expeditions they live chiefly by hunting, or on wild fruits and roots, with which the woods fupply them almoft every where.

They can bear hunger and thirft for feveral days, without flackening, on that account, their perfeverance in any propofed enterprize.

By conftant practice in hunting, they learn to fhoot with great fkill, either with bows, or firearms; and to fteal unperceived upon their prey, purfuing the tracts of men and beafts, which would be imperceptible to an European. They can run for a whole day without halting, when flying from an enemy, or when fent on any meffage. They fteer, as if by inftinct, thro' tracklefs woods, and with aftonifhing patience can lie whole days motionlefs in ambufh to furprife an enemy, efteeming no labour or perfeverance too painful to obtain their ends.

They

They besmear their bodies with bear's greafe, which defends them against rains and damps, as well as against the stings of Muskitoes and Gnats. It likewife supples their limbs, and makes them as slippery as the antient gladiators, who could not be held fast when feized in fight.

Plain food, constant exercife, and living in the open air, preferve them healthy and vigorous.

They are powerfully excited to war by the custom established among them, of paying distinguished honours to warriors.

They fight only when they think to have the advantage, but cannot be forced to it, being sure by their speed to elude the most eager pursuit.

Their drefs confifts of the skins of fome wild beast, or a blanket, a shirt either of linen, or of dreffed skins, a breech clout, leggins, reaching half way up the thigh, and fastened to a belt, with mokawsons on their feet. They ufe no ligatures that might obstruct the circulation of their blood, or agility of their limbs. They shave their head, referving only a small tuft of hair on the top; and slit the outer part of the ears, to which, by weights,

weights, they give a circular form, extending it down to their fhoulders.

They adorn themfelves with ear and nofe rings, bracelets of filver and wampum, and paint their faces with various colours. When they prepare for an engagement they paint themfelves black, and fight naked.

Their arms are a fufil, or rifle, a powder horn, a fhot pouch, a tomahawk, and a fcalping knife hanging to their neck.

When they are in want of firearms, they fupply them by a bow, a fpear, or a death hammer, which is a fhort club made of hard wood.

Their ufual utenfils are a kettle, a fpoon, a looking glafs, an awl, a fteel to ftrike fire, fome paint, a pipe and tobacco-pouch. For want of tobacco, they fmoke fome particular leaves, or the bark of a willow; which is almoft their continual occupation.

Thus lightly equipped do the favages lie in wait to attack, at fome difficult pafs, the European foldier, heavily accoutred, haraffed by a tedious march, and encumbered with an unwieldy convoy.

Experience

EXPERIENCE has convinced us that it is not our intereft to be at war with them; but if, after having tried all means to avoid it, they force us to it, (which in all probability will often happen) we fhould endeavour to fight them upon more equal terms, and regulate our manœuvres upon thofe of the enemy we are to engage, and the nature of the country we are to act in.

IT does not appear from our accounts of Indian wars, that the favages were as brave formerly as we have found them of late; which muft be imputed to their unexpected fucceffes againft our troops on fome occafions, particularly in 1755; and from the little refiftance they have fince met with from defencelefs inhabitants.

IT is certain that even at this day, they feldom expofe their perfons to danger, and depend entirely upon their dexterity in concealing themfelves during an engagement, never appearing openly, unlefs they have ftruck their enemies with terror, and have thereby rendered them incapable of defence. —— From whence it may be inferred that, if they were beat two or three times, they would lofe that confidence infpired by fuccefs, and be lefs inclined to engage in wars which might end fatally

for

for them. But this cannot reafonably be expected, till we have troops trained to fight them in their own way, with the additional advantage of European courage and difcipline.

ANY deviation from our eftablifhed military fyftem would be needlefs, if valour, zeal, order and good conduct, were fufficient to fubdue this light-footed enemy. Thefe qualities are confpicuous in our troops; but they are too heavy, and indeed too valuable, to be employed alone in a deftructive fervice for which they were never intended. They require the affiftance of lighter corps, whofe drefs, arms and exercifes, fhould be adapted to this new kind of war.

THIS opinion is fupported by the example of many warlike nations, of which I beg leave to mention the following.

THE learned Jefuit† who has obliged the world with a treatife on the military affairs of the ancient Romans, tells us, from Salluft§, that this wife
nation

---

† Vid. Joannis Antonii Valtrini Lbr, de re milit, Vet. Rom.

§ Neque enim Romanis fuperbia unquam obftitit, quo minus aliena inftituta, fi modo proba fuiffent, imitarentur; et quod
ubique

nation, our masters in the art of war, were never hindered even by the pride of empire, from imitating any foreign maxim or institution, provided it was good; and that they carefully adopted into their own practice whatever they found useful in that of their allies or enemies; so that by receiving some things from one, and some from another, they greatly improved a system even originally excellent.

THE defeat of Antony and Crassus by the Parthians, of Curio by the Numidians, and many other instances, convinced the Romans that their legions, who had conquered so many nations, were not fit to engage light-troops, which, harrassing them continually, evaded all their endeavours to bring them to a close engagement; and it is probable that if Julius Cæsar had not been assassinated, when he was preparing to march against the same Parthians, to wipe off the reproach of the former defeats, he would have added to his legions a greater number of light troops, formed upon the principles and method of that nation, and have left us useful lessons for the conduct of a war against our savages.

---

ubique apud socios vel hostes idoneum visum esset, cum studio domi exsequerentur. — Aliaque ab aliis accepta, ipsi longe facere meliora quæ quidem digna statuissent.

THAT

With the Savages of North-America. 103

THAT he did not think the attack of irregular troops contemptible, appears clearly in several parts of his commentaries, and particularly in the African war. The various embarraffments he met with from the enemy he had then to deal with, neceffarily call to our mind many fimilar circumftances in the courfe of our wars with the Indians; and the pains he took to inftruct his foldiers to ftand and repel the fkirmifhes of the nimble Africans, may furnifh inftruction to us in our military operations againft the favage Americans.

WE are told that while Cæfar was on his march " to Scipio's* quarters, the enemy's horfe and " light-armed infantry, rifing all at once from an " ambufcade, appeared upon the hills, and attacked
" his

*Labienus, Afraniufque cum omni equitatu, levique armatura, ex infidiis adorti agmini Cæfaris extremo fe offerunt, atque ex collibus primis exfiftunt. — Primo impetu legionum equitatus, levis armatura hoftium nullo negotio loco pulfa et dejecta eft de colle. Quum jam Cæfar exiftimaffet hoftes pulfos deterritofque finem laceffendi facturos, et iter cœptum pergere cœpiffet; iterum celeriter ex proximis collibus erumpunt; atque in Cæfaris legionarios impetum faciunt Numidæ, levifque armaturæ mirabili velocitate præditi; qui inter equites pugnabant, et una pariterque cum equitibus accurere et refugere comfueverant. Hoc fæpius, facerent, &c. — Cæfaris autem non ampliustres, aut quatuor milites veterani, fi fe convertiffent, et pila viribus contorta in Numidas infeftos conjeciffent, amplius duorum millium numero ad unum terga vertebant;

"his rear. His legions forming themselves, soon
"beat the enemy from the higher ground. And
"now thinking all safe, he begins to pursue his
"march. But immediately the enemy break forth
"from the neighbouring hills; and the Numidians,
"with their light-armed foot, who are wonderfully
"nimble, always mixing and keeping equal pace
"with the cavalry in charging or retiring, fall
"afresh on the Roman foot. Thus they fre-
"quently renewed the charge, and still retired when
"he endeavoured to bring them to close engage-
"ment. If but two or three of his veterans faced
"about and cast their piles with vigour, two thou-
"sand of the enemy would fly, then returning
"rally again, making it their business to harrass
"his march, and to press upon his rear, following

---

vertebant; ac rursus ad aciem passim, conversis equis, se colligebant, atque in spatio consequebantur, et jacula in Legionarios conjiciebant.

 CÆSAR contra ejusmodi hostium genera copias suas, non ut imperator exercitum veteranum, victoremque maximis rebus gestis, sed ut lanista tirones gladiatores condocefacere: quo pede sese reciperent ab hoste, &c. — Mirifice enim hostium levis armatura anxium exercitum ejus atque sollicitum habebat; quia et equites deterrebat prœlium inire, propter equorum interritum; quod eos jaculis interficiebat; et legionarium militem defatigabat, propter velocitatem. Gravis enim armatura miles simul atque ab his infectatus constiterat, in eosque impetum fecerat, illi veloci cursu facile periculum vitabant.

at

"at some distance and throwing their darts at the
"legions.

"CÆSAR, having so subtil an enemy to deal
"with, instructed his soldiers, not like a general
"who had been victorious in the most arduous
"exploits, but as a fencing-master† would instruct
"his scholars; teaching them with what pace to
"retreat from the enemy, and how to return to
"the charge; how far to advance, and how far to
"retire; and likewise in what place and manner to
"cast their piles. For their light-armed infantry
"gave him the greatest uneasiness, deterring his
"troopers from meeting them, by killing their
"horses with their javelins, and wearying his
"legions by their swiftness. For whenever his
"heavy-armed foot faced about, and endeavoured
"to return their charge, they quickly avoided the
"danger by flight."

But without going back to the ancients, we have seen this maxim adopted in our days. Marshal de Saxe finding the French army harrassed by the Hussars and other Austrian light troops, formed also several corps of them of different

†Lanista, in Latin, is an instructor of gladiators, which in English can only be translated a "Fencing-master."

kinds;

kinds; and the king of Pruffia in his firft war introduced them into his army, and has augmented and employed them ever fince with fuccefs. We have ourfelves made ufe of them in the two laft wars in Europe: But the light troops wanted in America muft be trained on different principles. The enemies we have to deal with, are infinitely more active and dangerous than the Huffars and Pandours; or even the Africans above-mentioned. For the American favages, after their rapid incurfions, retreat to their towns, at a great diftance from our fettlements, through thickety woods almoft impenetrable to our heavy and unwieldy corps, compofed of foldiers loaded with cloaths, baggage and provifions, who, when fatigued by a long march, muft be a very unequal match to engage the nimble favage in woods, which are his native element.

ANOTHER unavoidable incumbrance, in our expeditions, arifes from the provifions and baggage of the army, for which a road muft be opened, and bridges thrown over rivers and fwamps. This creates great labour, retards and weakens the line of march, and keeps the troops tied to a convoy which they cannot lofe fight of, without expofing it to become a prey to a vigilant enemy, continually hovering about to feize every advantage.

AN

An European, to be a proper judge of this kind of war, muſt have lived ſome time in the vaſt foreſts of America; otherwiſe he will hardly be able to conceive a continuity of woods without end. In ſpite of his endeavours, his imagination will betray him into an expectation of open and clear grounds, and he will be apt to calculate his manœuvres accordingly, too much upon the principles of war in Europe.

Let us ſuppoſe a perſon, who is entirely unacquainted with the nature of this ſervice, to be put at the head of an expedition in America. We will further ſuppoſe that he has made the diſpoſitions uſual in Europe for a march, or to receive an enemy; and that he is then attacked by the ſavages. He cannot diſcover them, tho' from every tree, log or buſh, he receives an inceſſant fire, and obſerves that few of their ſhot are loſt. He will not heſitate to charge thoſe inviſible enemies, but he will charge in vain. For they are as cautious to avoid a cloſe engagement, as indefatigable in harraſſing his troops; and notwithſtanding all his endeavours, he will ſtill find himſelf ſurrounded by a circle of fire, which, like an artificial horizon, follows him every where.

Unable

UNABLE to rid himſelf of an enemy who never ſtands his attacks, and flies when preſſed, only to return upon him again with equal agility and vigour; he will ſee the courage of his heavy troops droop, and their ſtrength at laſt fail them by repeated and ineffectual efforts.

HE muſt therefore think of a retreat, unleſs he can force his way thro' the enemy. But how is this to be effected? his baggage and proviſions are unloaded and ſcattered, part of his horſes and drivers killed, others diſperſed by fear, and his wounded to be carried by ſoldiers already fainting under the fatigue of a long action. The enemy, encouraged by his diſtreſs, will not fail to encreaſe the diſorder, by preſſing upon him on every ſide, with redoubled fury and ſavage howlings.

HE will probably form a circle or a ſquare, to keep off ſo daring an enemy, ready at the leaſt opening to fall upon him with the deſtructive tomahawk: but theſe diſpoſitions, tho' a tolerable ſhift for defence, are neither proper for an attack, nor a march thro' the woods. ——

THIS is not an imaginary ſuppoſition, but the true ſtate of an engagement with the Indians, experienced

experienced by the troops who have fought againſt them. Neither is there any thing new or extraordinary in this way of fighting, which ſeems to have been common to moſt Barbarians†.

WHAT is then to be done to extricate our little army from impending deſtruction?

THIS is a problem which I do not pretend to reſolve. But as every man would, in ſimilar circumſtances, determine himſelf ſome way or other, I will propoſe my own ſentiments, founded upon ſome obſervations which I believe invariable in all engagements with ſavages.

THE firſt, that their general maxim is to ſurround their enemy.

THE ſecond, that they fight ſcattered, and never in a compact body.

THE third, that they never ſtand their ground when attacked, but immediately give way, to return to the charge.

---

† Vid. Cæſ. Comm. lib. V. de bello Gallico, et lib. II de bello civili.

THESE

THESE principles being admitted, it follows——

1ſt. THAT the troops deſtined to engage Indians, muſt be lightly cloathed, armed, and accoutred.

2d. THAT having no reſiſtance to encounter in the attack or defence, they are not to be drawn up in cloſe order, which would only expoſe them without neceſſity to a greater loſs.

AND, laſtly, that all their evolutions muſt be performed with great rapidity; and the men enabled by exerciſe to purſue the enemy cloſely, when put to flight, and not give them time to rally.

THESE remarks will explain the reaſons of the alterations propoſed in the formation of a corps of troops, for the ſervice of the woods. It is not, however, to be expected that this method will remove all obſtacles, or that thoſe light troops can equal the ſavages in patience, and activity; but, with diſcipline and practice, they may in a great meaſure ſupply the want of theſe advantages, and by keeping the enemy at a diſtance afford great relief and ſecurity to the main body.

SECTION

SECTION II.

GENERAL IDEA OF AN ESTABLISHMENT OF LIGHT TROOPS FOR THE SERVICE OF THE WOODS.

I SHALL only venture a few notions fuggefted by experience upon this fubject, chiefly with a view to recommend it to the confideration of perfons capable of propofing a proper method of forming fuch an eftablifhment: and, in order to be better underftood, I will fuppofe a corps of 500 men to be raifed and difciplined for the woods, befides two troops of light horfe, to which a company of artificers might be added. The fitteft men for that fervice would be the natives of America bred upon the frontiers, and inlifted between the age of 15 and 20 years, to be difcharged between 30 and 35.

CLOATHING.

THE cloathing of a foldier for the campaign might confift of a fhort coat of brown cloth, lappelled, and without plaits; a ftrong tanned fhirt,

fhort

short trowsers, leggins, mokawsons or shoe packs, a sailor's hat, a blanket, a knapsack for provisions, and an oiled surtout† against the rain. To this might be added, in winter quarters or time of peace, three white shirts and stocks, with a flannel waistcoat.

ARMS.

† The following Watch-coat was contrived by an officer, whose name I do not remember, But instead of the oiled linen to be put under the hat, a cap might perhaps answer better. He writes as follows, viz.

"As the Indian war will require frequent incursions into a "wild country, where a man sick or wounded, is in several respects "more detrimental to the service than a man killed, every thing "that may contribute to the health of the men is of moment.

"In this view, I propose a sort of surtout, to preserve men, in "a great measure, both from wet and cold.

"Take a large checked shirt, of about half a crown sterling "per yard, for it should be pretty fine; cut off the wrist-bands, "and continue the opening of the breast down to the bottom; "sew up the sides from the gussets downwards; rip out the gath-"ers in the fore parts of the collar as far as the shoulder straps, "and resew it plain to the collar.

"The shirt will then become a sort of watch-coat like a bed-"gown, with very wide sleeves.

"Take a quantity of linseed oil, and boil it gently till one half "is dimished, to which put a small quantity of litharge of gold, "and when it is well incorporated with the oil, lay it on with a "brush upon the watch-coat, so that it shall be every where "equally wet.

"I suppose the watch-coat, hung in a garret, or other covered "place, and so suspended by crooked pins and pack threads in the "extremities of the sleeves and edges of the collar, that one part
"shall

ARMS.

Their arms, the beſt that could be made, ſhould be ſhort fuſils and ſome rifles, with bayonets in the form of a dirk, to ſerve for a knife; with powder horns and ſhot pouches, ſmall hatchets and leathern bottles for water.

" ſhall not touch another. In a ſhort time, if the weather is
" good, it will be dry; when a ſecond mixture of the ſame kind
" ſhould be laid on with a bruſh as before. When the ſecond
" coat of painting is dry, the greaſe will not come off, and the
" ſurtout is an effectual preſervative from rain; it is very light to
" carry, and being pretty full on the back, will not only keep the
" man dry, but alſo his pack and ammunition.

" The ſleeves are left long and wide, to receive the butt end of
" a firelock (ſecured) and to cover it below the lock. The coat
" is double breaſted to be lapped over, according to which ſide
" the rain drives. A man will be kept dry by one of theſe ſur-
" touts as far as the knees. If, from the vicinity of the enemy, it
" is improper to make fires at night, he may place his pack on a
" ſtone, and, ſitting upon it, change his ſhoes and leggins, and, if
" he pleaſes, wrap his blanket round his legs and feet, then draw-
" ing the watch-coat cloſe to his body, it will keep him warm, as
" no air can paſs through it, and, leaning againſt the trunk of a
" tree, he may paſs a tolerable night, both warm and dry.

" It would be of ſervice to have a ſmall piece of the ſame
" oiled linen to put under the hat or cap to carry the rain down
" to the watchcoat or ſurtout, otherwiſe whatever wet ſoaks
" through the hat or cap, will run down the neck, and thereby,
" in ſome meaſure, defeat the deſign of the watch-coat.

" Perhaps it might be useful to mix ſome dark or greeniſh
" colour with the oil of the ſecond coating, to make the watch-
" coat leſs remarkable in the woods."

EXERCISES.

EXERCISES.

The foldiers being raifed, cloathed, and formed into companies under proper officers, muft, before they are armed, be taught to keep themfelves clean, and to drefs in a foldier-like manner. This will raife in them a becoming fpirit, give them a favourable opinion of their profeffion, and preferve their health. [The firft thing they are to learn is to Walk well, afterwards to Run; and, in order to excite emulation, fmall premiums might from time to time be given to thofe who diftinguifh themfelves. They muft then run in ranks, with open files, and wheel in that order, at firft flowly, and by degrees increafe their fpeed: this evolution is difficult, but of the utmoft confequence to fall unexpectedly upon the flank of the enemy. They are to difperfe and rally at given fignals; and particular colours fhould be given to each company, for them to rally by; the men muft be ufed to leap † over logs and ditches, and to carry burthens proportioned to their ftrength.|

When

---

† Vegetius gives an account of many fimilar exercifes, which the Romans found neceffary to eftablifh among their military. Miles fylvam cædebat, æftivis temporibus natabat, ad palum dimicabat, faltabat, currebat. Exempla hujus exercitationis crebra funt apud Livium. Sic ille de Scipione Africano, 3 decad. lib. VI.

WHEN the young foldiers are perfect in thefe exercifes, they may receive their arms, with which they are to perform the former evolutions in all forts of grounds. They will next be taught to handle their arms with dexterity; and, without lofing time upon trifles, to load and fire very quick, ftanding, kneeling, or lying on the ground. They are to fire at a mark without a reft, and not fuffered to be too long in taking aim. Hunting and fmall premiums will foon make them expert markfmen.

THEY ought to learn to fwim, pufhing at the fame time their cloaths, arms, and ammunition before them, on a fmall raft; and to make ufe of fnow fhoes. They muft then be fet to work, and be taught to throw up an intrenchment, open a trench, make fafcines, clays and gabions; likewife to fall trees, fquare logs, faw planks, make canoes, carts, ploughs, hand and wheel barrows, fhingles and clap-boards, cafks, batteaus and bridges, and to build log houfes, ovens, &c.

VI. " Primo die legiones in armis IV. millium fpatio decurre-
" runt. Secundo die arma curare et tergere ante tentoria juffit.
" Tertio die fudibus inter fe in modum juftæ pugnæ concurrerent,
" præpilatifque miffilibus jaculati funt. Quarto die quies data.
" Quinto iterum in armis decurfum eft."—Quibus porro modis obviam eatur elephantis. Veget. lib. III. cap. 24.

BY

By example and practice, the moſt ingenious among them will ſoon become tolerable good carpenters, joyners, wheelwrights, coopers, armourers, ſmiths, maſons, brickmakers, ſaddlers, taylors, butchers, bakers, ſhoemakers, curriers, &c.

LIGHT HORSE and DOGS.

I SAID that, to compleat this eſtabliſhment, they ſhould have two troops of light horſe, ſuppoſed of 50 men each, officers included. The men are to perform the ſame exerciſes as the foot, and afterwards be taught to ride, and particularly to be very alert at mounting and diſmounting with their arms in their hands, to gallop through the woods, up and down hills, and leap over logs and ditches.

THE horſes ought to be bought up on the frontiers, where they are bred and uſed to feed in the woods, and are ſtrong and hardy. They are to be thoroughly broke, made to ſtand fire, to ſwim over rivers, &c. their ſaddles and accoutrements very ſimple, ſtrong and light. The number of horſes might be reduced to one half, in time of peace, tho' they would be of little expence, as they might be bred and maintained without charge in the

the military fettlement. This corps fhould be equipped as the foot, having only a fhort rifle in lieu of a fufil, and a battle ax with a long handle, the only fort of arms they fhould make ufe of in the charge.

EVERY light horfe man ought to be provided with a Blood-hound, which would be ufeful to find out the enemies ambufhes, and to follow their tracts; they would feize the naked favages, or at leaft give time to the horfe men to come up with them; they would add to the fafety of the camp at night by difcovering any attempt to furprize it.

ARTIFICERS.

THE company of artificers fhould be compofed of the moft ufeful tradefmen, and ought to be maintained at all times for the inftruction of the foldiers, the ufe of the fettlement, or the fervice of the army, during the campaign. It will now be time to draw forth this military colony and remove them to the ground laid out for that ufe in the woods, and at a good diftance from the inhabitants. The nature of this fettlement will hereafter be more particularly defcribed.

NECESSITY

NECESSITY creating induſtry, our young ſoldiers will ſoon provide themſelves with the moſt uſeful articles, and in a couple of years be able to raiſe proviſions for themſelves.

WHILE the greateſt part would be employed in clearing the ground, fencing, ploughing, ſowing, planting, building and making utenſils and houſehold furniture, others might hunt with their officers, and remain a fortnight or a month out of the camp, without other proviſions than a little flour, and what they could procure by hunting and fiſhing: then to be relieved, and the whole trained up in that way.

THE military exerciſes muſt ſtill be kept up and practiced, and great care taken to inculcate and preſerve purity of manners, obedience, order and decency among the men, which will be found much eaſier in the woods than in the neighbourhood of towns.

IN order to make this military eſtabliſhment more generally uſeful; I would propoſe that the ſoldiers ſhould only receive a very ſmall part of their pay; leaving the remainder in the military cheſt.

THEIR accounts ſhould be ſettled every year, and

and when their fervices fhould intitle them to their difcharge, I could wifh that each of them had 200 acres of land given him, in a diftrict appropriated for that purpofe; and receiving then the whole ballance of pay due them, they would then be enabled to compleat their fettlement. This inftitution appears not only practicable, but eafy, if attended to with patience, affiduity and firmnefs. The plan I would propofe is as follows.

Method of forming fuch SETTLEMENTS upon the Frontiers, as might fupport themfelves during an INDIAN WAR.

LET us fuppofe a fettlement to be formed for one hundred families, compofed of five perfons each, upon an average.

LAY out upon a river or creek, if it can be found conveniently, a SQUARE of one thoufand feven hundred and fixty yards, or a mile for each fide.

THAT Square will contain - -	640 acres
Allowing for ftreets and public ufes 40 To half an acre for every houfe - 50 To one hundred lotts at five and half acres - - - 550	640 acres

THE

The four fides of the fquare meafure 7040 yards, which gives to each houfe about 70 yards front to ftockade, and the ground allowed for building will be 210 feet front, and about 100 feet deep.

An acre of ground will produce at leaft 30 bufhels of Indian corn. Therefore, two acres are fufficient to fupply five perfons, at the rate of twelve bufhels each perfon. Two other acres will be a pafture for cows and fheep, another acre for hay, to be fown with red clover. The remaining half acre may be laid out for a garden.

Round the town are the commons, of three miles fquare, containing, exclufive of the lots abovementioned, 5120 acres. On three fides of the town, five other Squares will be laid out of three fquare miles, containing 5760 acres each, one of which is referved for wood for the ufe of the Settlement; the other four to be divided into 25 out-lotts or plantations, of about 230 acres each, fo that in the four Squares, there will be one hundred fuch plantations, for the 100 families.

Another townfhip may be laid out joining this, upon the fame plan, and as many more as you please upon the fame line, without lofing any ground.

The

With the Savages of North-America. 121

1	1	5760 acres wood for the Town A	Townſhip A.
1	A	25 lotts of 230 acres 1	
	Commons		
2	B	2	Townſhip B.
2	Wood for the Town B		
3	Wood for the Town C	3	Townſhip C.
3	C		
4	D	4	Townſhip D.
4	Wood for the Town D		

The following is a rough ſketch of the whole.

Thus

Thus the town, A, has its commons, its woodland, and its 4 squares marked No. 1. each containing 25 plantations of 230 acres, as propoſed above. In like manner, the other towns, B, C, D, have their appurtenances reſpectively marked.

Let us now ſuppoſe this plan accompliſhed, and ſuch corps as theſe fully ſettled, trained and diſciplined, in the manner abovementioned; I would aſk whether any officer, entruſted with an expedition againſt the ſavages, would not chuſe to have them in his army? I may ſafely anſwer for all thoſe who have been employed in that ſervice, that they would prefer them to double the number of the beſt European troops. And when they had ſerved the time limited, namely from their 15th to their 35th year, what vaſt ſatisfaction would it be to pay over to them their ſhare of ſavings from the public cheſt; and, as a reward of their faithful toils, to veſt them and their heirs with their ſeveral plantations, which they would now be enabled to cultivate as their own? This proſpect would engage many people to enter their ſons, in ſuch corps; and thoſe veterans, when thus diſcharged, would not only be the means of forming and animating others by their example, but in caſe of a war would ſtill bravely maintain the property they

they had fo honorably acquired, and be the greateft fecurity of the frontier where they are fettled.

PREPARATIONS FOR AN EXPEDITION IN THE WOODS AGAINST SAVAGES.

It is not practicable to employ large bodies of troops againft Indians; the convoys neceffary for their fupport would be too cumberfome, and could neither be moved with eafe, nor protected. It would be better to fit out feveral fmall expeditions, than one too unwieldy: I will therefore fuppofe that a corps intended to act offenfively fhall not exceed the following proportions.

Two regiments of foot - - - - - 900
One battalion of hunters - - - - 500
Two troops of light horfe - - - - 100
One company of artificers - - - - 20
Drivers and neceffary followers - - - 280

In all 1800

The firft article to provide is the provifions, and next the carriages.

The daily ration of a foldier in the woods fhould confift of one pound and a half of meat (which

(which requires no carriage) and one pound of flour, with a gill of salt per week.

Upon that allowance 1800 men will require for fix months or 182 days — — } 327,600 lb. Flour.

    Allowing one fourth for
        accident — — — — — —   81,900

    For fix months   409,500 lb. Flour.

Meat for the fame time with a fourth part more for accidents, or 2048 beeves at 300 lb. each — — — — } 614,400 lb. Meat.

    Salt for 26 weeks — — —   182 Bufhels.

The above quantity would ferve the whole campaign, but one half would be fufficient to penetrate from the laft depofite into the heart of the enemy's country: therefore we fhall compute the carriages for this laft quantity only.

Every horfe carries about 150 lb. neat weight, therefore, to carry flour for three months or 204,750 lb. will require 1365 horfes.

Horses

With the Savages of North-America. 125

Horses for flour brought forward - -	1365
For 91 bufhels of falt - - - -	46
Ammunition - - - - -	50
Tents - - - - - -	50
Tools - - - - - -	50
Hofpital - - - - - -	20
Officers baggage and ftaff - - -	150
	1731

To reduce this exorbitant number of horfes, and the great expence attending it, I would propofe, for fuch parts of the country as would admit of it, to make ufe of carts, drawn each by four oxen, and carrying about 1300 lb. or fix barrels of flour. The above quantity of 204,750 lb. will then be carried by 160 carts drawn by - - - 640 oxen
Spare oxen with the army - - - - 384

The number of oxen wanted - 1024

THIS method would not be as expeditious as the carriage by horfes, and would require more time and attention in cutting the road, and bridging the fwampy places, &c. but, on the other hand, what an expence would be faved! and by killing the oxen in proportion as the flour is ufed, and abandoning

abandoning the carts, the convoy is daily reduced, and the grafs near the encampment will not be fo foon confumed, which is not the cafe with horfes, which muft equally be fed though unloaded. This is an object of confequence, particularly near the end of the campaign, when the fcarcity of fodder obliges to move the camps every day, and to place them in low and difadvantageous grounds.

I WOULD therefore incline for the ufe of carts, and they could be made before hand by the hunters and their artificers.

THE oxen fhould be bought in the provinces where the farmers make ufe of them in their works. One or two foldiers would drive the cart and take charge of the four oxen.

THERE are few rivers in North-America deep in fummer, and which thefe carts with high and broad wheels, could not ford; but if the contrary fhould happen, the carts, provifions and baggage, may be rafted over, or a bridge built. In a country full of timber, and with troops accuftomed to work, no river will ftop an army for a long time.

BY the above method, 3 or 400 horfes would be fufficient

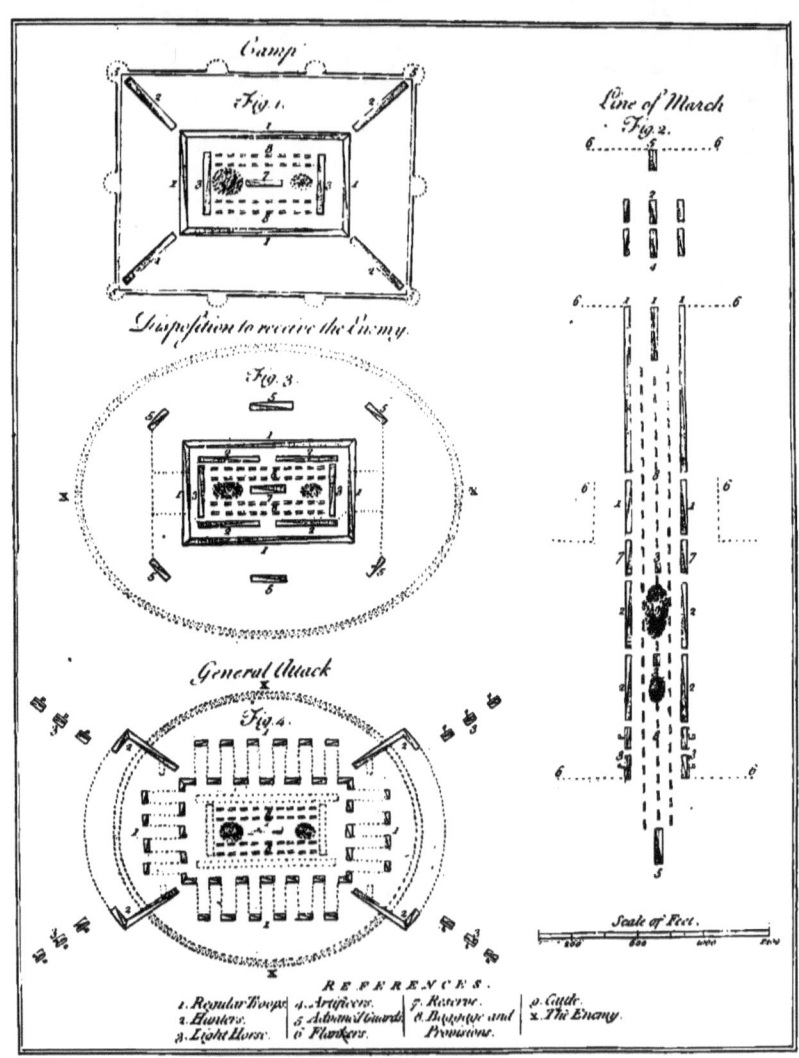

fufficient to carry the baggage, ammunition, tents, tools, &c.

EXPLANATION OF THE FOUR PLANS,
†PLATE II.
Reprefenting the different pofitions of our army in the woods.

ENCAMPMENT.

THE camp (Fig. 1) forms a parallellogram, of one thoufand by fix hundred feet. Eight hundred men of the regular troops (1) encamp on the four fides, which gives twenty-four feet to each tent, containing fix men. The light-horfe (3) encamp within the parallellogram. The referve (7) in the center.

THE provifions, ammunition, tools and ftores (8) and the cattle (9) are placed between the two troops of light-horfe and the referve. The hunters (2) encamp on the outfide diagonally at the four angles, being covered by redoubts (5) formed with kegs and bags of flour or fafcines. Befides thefe four redoubts, another is placed to the front, one

---
† See this Plate before Pag. 40.

to

to the rear, and two before each of the long faces of the camp, making in all ten advanced guards of 22 men each, and 7 centries, covered if poffible by breaft works of fafcines or provifions. Before the army lay down their arms, the ground is to be reconnoitred, and the guards pofted, who will immediately open a communication from one to the other to relieve the centries, and facilitate the paffage of rounds.

The centries upon the ammunition, provifions, head quarters, and all others in the infide of the camp are furnifhed from the referve. The officers, except the ftaff and commanders of corps, encamp on the line with their men.

The fires are made between the guards and camp, and put out in cafe of an attack in the night.

LINE of MARCH, Plate II. Fig. II.

Part of the hunters (2) in three divifions detaching fmall parties (5, 6) to their front and to their right and left, to fearch the woods and difcover the enemy.

The

THE artificers and ax-men (4) to cut a road for the convoy, and two paths on the right and left for the troops.

ONE hundred and fifty of the regular troops (1) in two files, who are to form the front of the fquare; thefe march in the center road.

Two hundred and fifty regulars (1) in one file by the right hand path; and 250 (1) by the left hand path, are to form the long faces.

THESE are followed by 150 regulars (1) in two files, who are to form the rear of the fquare.

THE referve (7) compofed of 100 regulars in two files.

THE reft of the hunters (2) in two files.

THE light horfe (3.)

THE rear guard (5) compofed of hunters, fol-'lows the convoy at fome diftance and clofes the march. The fcouting parties (6) who flank the line of march, are taken from the hunters and light horfe, and pofted as in plan (Fig. 2), fome orderly light

light horſe men, attend the General and field officers who command the grand diviſions, to carry their orders. Two guards of light horſe take charge of the cattle (9.)

The convoy (8) proceeds in the following order.

The tools and ammunition following the front column.

The baggage.

The cattle.

The proviſions.

The whole divided into Brigades, and the horſes two a breaſt.

DEFILES.

In caſe of a defile, the whole halt until the ground is reconnoitred, and the hunters have taken poſſeſſion of the heights. The center column then enters into the defile, followed by the right face; after them the convoy; then the left and rear face, with the reſerve, the light horſe, and the rear guard.

The

THE whole to form again as foon as the ground permits.

DISPOSITION TO RECEIVE THE ENEMY, Fig. (3).

THE whole halt to form the fquare or parallellogram, which is done thus. The two firft men of the center column ftand faft at two yards diftance. The two men following them, ftep forward and poft themfelves at two yards on the right and left. The others come to the front in the fame manner, till the two files have formed a rank, which is the front of the fquare.

THE rear face is formed by the two file-leaders turning to the center road, where having placed themfelves at two yards diftance, they face outwards, and are followed by their files, each man pofting himfelf on their right or left, and facing towards the enemy the moment he comes to his poft.

As foon as the front and rear are extended and formed, the two long faces, who have in the mean time faced outwards, join now the extremities of the two fronts and clofe the fquare †.

---

† Thefe evolutions muft be performed with celerity.

To REDUCE THE SQUARE.

THE right and left of the front, face to the center, where the two center men ſtand faſt. Upon the word "march" theſe ſtep forward and are replaced by the two next, who follow them, and ſo on; by which means, that front becomes again a column. The rear goes to the right about, and each of the two center men leads again to the ſide paths followed by the reſt.

WHILE the troops form, the light horſe and each diviſion of the convoy take the ground aſſigned to them within the ſquare, as if they were to encamp; and the horſes being unloaded, two parallel lines will be formed, with the bags and kegs of proviſions, to cover the wounded and the men unfit for action. The hunters take poſt on the moſt advantageous ground on the out ſide, and ſkirmiſh with the enemy, till the ſquare is formed; when, upon receiving their orders, they retire within the ſquare, where they take their poſt as in Fig. (3).

THE ſmall parties of rangers (5) who have flanked the line of march, remain on the outſide, to keep off the enemy and obſerve their motions.

WHEN

When the firing begins the troops will have orders to fall on their knees, to be lefs expofed till it is thought proper to attack.

The four faces, formed by the regular troops, are divided into platoons *chequered*. One half, compofed of the beft and moft active foldiers, is called the firft Firing, and the other half the fecond Firing.

The eight platoons at the angles are of the fecond Firing, in order to preferve the form of the fquare during the attack.

It is evident that, by this difpofition, the convoy is well covered, and the light troops, deftined for the charge, remain concealed; and as all unexpected events during an engagement are apt to ftrike terror, and create confufion, among the enemy, it is natural to expect that the favages will be greatly difconcerted at the fudden and unforefeen eruption, that will foon pour upon them from the infide of the fquare; and that, being vigoroufly attacked in front and flank at the fame time, they will neither be able to refift, nor, when once broke, have time to rally, fo as to make another ftand. This may be effected in the following manner.

GENERAL

GENERAL ATTACK, Fig. IV.

The Regulars (1) ſtand faſt.

The hunters (2) ſally out, in four columns, thro' the intervals of the front and rear of the ſquare, followed by the light horſe (3) with their bloodhounds. The intervals of the two columns who attack in the front, and of thoſe who attack in the rear, will be cloſed by the little parties of rangers (5) poſted at the angles of the ſquare, each attack forming in that manner, three ſides of a parallelogram. In that order they run to the enemy (X) and having forced their way through their circle, fall upon their flanks; by wheeling to their right and left, and charging with impetuoſity. The moment they take the enemy in flank, the Firſt Firing of the regular troops march out briſkly and attack the enemy in front. The platoons detached in that manner from the two ſhort faces, proceed only about one hundred yards to their front, where they halt to cover the ſquare, while the reſt of the troops who have attacked purſue the enemy, till they are totally diſperſed, not giving them time to recover themſelves.

The

THE fick and wounded, unable to march or ride, are tranfported in litters made of flour bags, through which two long poles are paffed, and kept afunder by two fticks, tied acrofs beyond the head and feet to ftretch the bag. Each litter is carried by two horfes——

THESE remarks might have been extended to many other cafes that may occur in the courfe of a campaign or of an engagement, but it is hoped this fketch will be fufficient to evince the neceffity of fome alteration in our ordinary method of proceeding in an Indian war.

APPENDIX I.

CONSTRUCTION OF FORTS AGAINST INDIANS.

AS we have not to guard here againſt cannon, the ſyſtem of European fortifications may be laid aſide, as expenſive, and not anſwering the purpoſe. Forts againſt Indians, being commonly remote from our ſettlements, require a great deal of room to lodge a ſufficient quantity of ſtores and proviſions, and at the ſame time ought to be defenſible with one half of their compleat garriſons, in caſe of detachments or convoys.

I AM therefore of opinion that a ſquare or pentagon, with a block-houſe of brick or ſtone* at every angle, joined by a wall flanked by the block-houſes, would be the beſt defence againſt ſuch

---

*Experience has demonſtrated that fortifications made of wood decay very ſoon, and are on that account of conſiderable expence.

enemies.

enemies. A ditch from feven to eight feet deep might be added, with loop holes in the cellars of the block-houfes fix feet from the ground, to defend the ditch.

Along the infide of the curtains the traders might build houfes and ftores, covered as well as the block-houfes with tiles, or flate, to guard againft fire arrows. There will remain a fpacious area for free air and ufe, in which as well as in the ditch, gardens might be made and wells dug.

The powder magazines might be placed in the center of the area, keeping only a fmall quantity of cartridges in each block-houfe for prefent ufe.

The garrifons of fuch forts would be free from furprizes, even if they had no centries, for nothing can get at them, while the doors are well bolted and barred.

Some reasons for keeping possession of our large forts in the Indian country.

As thefe forts have been one of the caufes of the laft war and are a great eye-fore to the favages, they have bent their chief efforts againft them; and

Appendix I. 139

and therefore, while thus employed, they have been lefs able to diftrefs our fettlements. Our forts keep the Indian towns at a great diftance from us. Fort-Pitt has effectually driven them beyond the Ohio, and made them remove their fettlements at leaft 60 miles further weftward. Was it not for thefe forts, they would fettle clofe on our borders, and in time of war infeft us every day in fuch numbers as would over-power the thin inhabitants fcattered on our extenfive frontier. The farmer unable to fow or reap would foon fall back on our chief towns, or quit the country for want of bread. In either cafe, what would be the fate of the large towns burthened with the whole country, and deprived of fubfiftance and of the materials of trade and export?

THE deftruction of thefe forts being, in time of war, the chief aim of the favages, they gather about them to diftrefs the garrifons, and to attack the convoys; thereby giving us an opportunity to fight them in a body, and to ftrike a heavy blow, which otherwife they would never put in our power, as their advantage lies in furprizes, which are beft effected by fmall numbers. Experience has convinced them that it is not in their power to break thofe fhackles, and therefore it is not probable that

that they will renew the attempt; and our pofts will continue a check upon them, and fave the difficulty and expence of taking poft again in their country. Our forts are likewife the proper places for trade, which being clofely infpected, it will be eafy for us to limit their fupplies, to fuch commodities as they cannot turn againft us, and to put a fpeedy ftop to all juft caufes of complaints, by giving immediate redrefs.

A FEW forts, with ftrong garrifons, I fhould judge to be of more fervice than a greater number weakly guarded. In the laft war we loft all our fmall pofts; but our more confiderable ones, Detroit and Fort-Pitt, refifted all the efforts of the favages, by the ftrength of their garrifons.

APPENDIX

APPENDIX II.

THE following Paper was written by an Officer well acquainted with the places he defcribes; and is thought worthy of a place here, as every thing is material which can encreafe our knowledge of the vaft countries ceded to us and of the various nations that inhabit them.

ACCOUNT OF THE FRENCH FORTS ceded to GREAT BRITAIN in LOUISIANA.

THE fettlement of the Illinois being in 40 degrees of latitude, is 500 leagues from New-Orleans by water and 350 by land.

THE moft proper time of the year for going there, is the beginning of February. The waters of the Miffifippi are then high, and the country being overflowed, there is lefs to fear from the favages, who are hunting in that feafon.

THE

Appendix II.

THE encampments fhould be on the left of the river, as the enemies are on the right, and cannot have a fufficient number of crafts to crofs if their party is large.

THEY generally attack at day-break, or at the time of embarking.

THE inhabitants might bring provifions half way, if they were allowèd good pay.

THE Delawares and Shawanefe lie near Fort Du Quefne,† which is about 500 leagues from the Illinois. The Wiandots and Ottawas, (who are at the Detroit) are about 250 leagues from the Illinois by land. And the Miamis about 200 by land.

NEVERTHELESS as intelligence is carried very faft by the Savages, and as all the nations with whom we are at war, can come by the Ohio,‡ we muft be vigilant to prevent a furprize.

THE

---

† So the French formerly called what is now Fort Pitt.

‡ Part of the navigation of the Ohio, from Fort-Pitt is defcribed as follows, viz.

That the difficult part of the river is from Fort-Pitt about 50 or 60 miles downwards. There are 52 iflands between Fort-Pitt and the lower Shawanefe town on Scioto; and none of them difficult

Appendix II. 143

THE mouth of the Ohio, in the Miffifippi, is 35 leagues from the Illinois.

THIRTEEN leagues from the Miffifippi, on the left of the Ohio, is Fort Maffiac, or Affumption, built in 1757, a little below the mouth of the river Cherokee†. It is only a ftockade, with four baftions and eight pieces of cannon. It may contain 100 men. In four days one may go by land, from this fort to the Illinois.

IT is of confequence for the Englifh to preferve it, as it fecures the communication between the Illinois and Fort-Pitt.

FORT Vincennes, which is the laft poft belonging to Louifiana, is upon the river Ouabache‡, 60

---

difficult to pafs in the night, but one at the mouth of Mufkingham, occafioned by a number of trees lying in the channel. From the lower Shawanefe Town to the falls, there are but 8 or 9 iflands. At the falls, the river is very broad, with only one paffage on the eaft fide, in which there is water enough at all feafons of the year to pafs without difficulty. Below the falls, the navigation is every way clear down to the Miffifippi.

† River Cherokee falls into the Ohio about 800 miles below Fort-Pitt. This river is in general wide and fhoal up to the fouth mountain, paffable only with bark canoes, after which it grows very fmall.

‡ Ouabache or Wabafh empties itfelf into the Ohio about 60 miles above the Cherokee river, on the oppofite or weft fide.

leagues

leagues from its conflux with the Ohio. It is a
fmall ftockade fort, in which there may be about
20 foldiers. There are alfo a few inhabitants.
The foil is extremely fertile, and produces plenty
of corn and tobacco.

THE diftance from this fort to the Illinois, is
155 leagues by water. And it may be travelled
by land in fix days.

THE nation of favages living at this poft is
called Pianquicha. It can furnifh 60 warriors.

ALTHO' we do not occupy Fort Vincennes at
prefent, yet it would be of the utmoft confequence for us to fettle it, as there is a communication from it with Canada, by going up the
Ouabache.

FROM this poft to the Ouachtanons is 60
leagues, and from thence to the Miamis (ftill
going up the Ouabache) is 60 leagues further;
then there is a portage of fix leagues to the river
Miamis, and you go down that river 24 leagues
to Lake Erie.

MR. DAURBY went by that route in 1759 from
the

Appendix II. 145

the Illinois to Venango ‖, with above 400 men, and two hundred thousand weight of flour.

THIRTY-FIVE leagues from the mouth of the Ohio, in going up the Miffifippi, on the right, is the river Kafkafquias. Two leagues up this river, on the left, is the fettlement of the Kafkafquias, which is the moft confiderable of the Illinois.

THERE is a fort built upon the height on the other fide of the river, over againft Kafkafquias;

‖ By the above paper the rout is given up the Miffifippi, part of the Ohio, and up the Ouabache to Fort Vincennes, and likewife to the Illinois. Again from Vincennes and the Ouachtanons by water, on the wefterly communication to the Miamis portage, then by water down that river by the eafterly rout into Lake Erie, proceeding as far as Prefqu' Ifle, then by the 15 m. portage into Buffalo or Beef river, lately called French creek, then down the fame to Venango on the Ohio. In order, therefore, to carry this rout ftill further, we shall continue it from Venango to the mouth of Juniata in Sufquehannah, which brings it within the fettled parts of Pennfylvania, viz.

From Venango to Licking creek, 10 miles. To Toby's creek, 13. To a fmall creek, 1. To the parting of the road, 5. To a large run, 3. To Leycaumeyhoning, 9. To Pine creek, 7. To Chuckcaughting, 8. To Weeling creek, 4. To the croffing of ditto, 4. To a miry fwamp, 8. To the head of Sufquehanna, 10. To Meytauning creek, 18. To Clear Field creek, 6. To the top of Allegheny, 1. To the other fide ditto, 6. To Beaver dams, 5. To Franks town, 5. To the Canoe place, 6. To the mouth of Juniatta, 110. Total 239 miles.

which,

which, as the river is narrow, commands and protects the town.

I don't know how many guns there may be, nor how many men it may contain. There may be about 400 inhabitants.

The Illinois Indians, called Kafkafquias, are settled half a league from the town; and are able to turn out 100 warriors. They are very lazy and great drunkards.

Six leagues from Kafkafquias, on the bank of the Miffifippi, is Fort Chartres, built of ftone, and can contain 300 foldiers. There may be 20 cannon at moft, and about 100 inhabitants round Chartres.

The Illinois Indians at that place, who are called Metchis, can furnifh 40 warriors.

Between the Kafkafquias, and Fort Chartres, is a fmall village, called *La prairie du Rocher* (the Rock Meadow) containing about 50 white inhabitants; but there is neither fort nor favages.

Near Fort Chartres is a little village, in which
is

is about a score of inhabitants. Here are neither savages nor fort.

FIFTEEN leagues from Fort Chartres, going up the Missisippi, is the village of the Casquiars. There is a small stockade fort; I don't know if there is any cannon. There may be about 100 inhabitants.

THE Illinois Indians living near this village are called Casquiars, and can turn out 60 warriors.

I COMPUTE that there are about 300 Negroes at the Illinois.

THE country of the Illinois is fertile, producing good wheat and corn. All kinds of European fruits succeed there surprizingly well, and they have wild grapes with which they make tolerable wine. Their beer is pretty good.

THERE are mines of lead, and some salt. They make sugar of maple, and there are stone quarries.

APPENDIX

APPENDIX III.

ROUT from PHILADELPHIA to FORT-PITT.

	Miles	Qrs.	Per.
From PHILADELPHIA to Lancafter	66	0	38
to Carlifle	55	0	00
to Shippenfburgh	22	0	00
to Fort Loudoun	24	3	00
to Fort Littleton	17	3	00
to the crofling of the Juniata	18	3	00
to Fort Bedford	14	3	00
to the croffing of Stoney creek	29	0	39
to Fort Ligonier	20	1	43
to Fort Pitt	56	0	00
	324	2	40

APPENDIX IV.

NUMBER of INDIAN TOWNS, fituated on and near the Ohio River, and its branches, with their diftances from Fort-Pitt, and the diftances of the principal branches from each other at their conflux with the Ohio.

FIRST ROUT about N. N. W.

	Diftance from one another. Miles	Diftance from Fort-Pitt. Miles
From FORT PITT to KufhkufkiesTown on Big Beaver-Creek		45
up the eaft branch of Beaver-Creek to Shaningo	15	60
up ditto to Pematuning	12	72
to Mohoning on the Weft branch of Beaver Creek	32	104
up the branch to Salt Lick	10	114
to Cayahoga River	32	146
to Ottawas town on Cayahoga	10	156

SECOND

Appendix IV.

	Diftance from one another.	Diftance from Fort-Pitt.
SECOND ROUT W. N. W.	Miles	Miles
From FORT PITT to the mouth of Big Beaver-Creek		25
to Tufcarawas	91	116
to Mohickon John's Town	50	166
to Junundat or Wyandot town	46	212
to Sandufky	4	216
to Junqueindundeh	24	240

THIRD ROUT about W. S. W.

From FORT PITT to the Forks of the Mufkingham		128
to Bullet's Town on Mufkingham	6	134
to Waukatamike	10	144
to King Beaver's Town on the heads of the Hockhocking	27	171
to the lower Shawanefe Town on Sioto River	40	211
to the Salt Lick town on the heads of Sioto	25	236
to the Miamis Fort	190	429

FOURTH

Appendix IV.

FOURTH ROUT down the Ohio; general courſe about S. W.

	Diſtance from one another. Miles	Diſtance from Fort-Pitt. Miles
By water from FORT PITT to the mouth of Big Beaver Creek		27
to the mouth of Little Beaver Creek	12	39
to the mouth of Yellow Creek	10	49
to the two Creeks	18	67
to Weeling	6	73
to Pipe Hill	12	85
to the long Reach	30	115
to the foot of the Reach	18	133
to the mouth of Muſkingham River	30	163
to the little Canhawa river	12	175
to the mouth of Hockhocking river	13	188
to the mouth of Letort's creek	40	228
to Kiſkeminetas	33	261
to the mouth of big Canhawa or new river	8	269
to the mouth of big Sandy creek	40	309
to the mouth of Sioto river	40	349
to the mouth of big Salt Lick river	30	379
to the Iſland	20	399

to the

	Distance from one another.	Distance from Fort-Pitt.
	Miles	Miles
to the mouth of little Mineamie or Miammee † river	55	454
to big Miammee or Rocky river	30	484
to the Big Bones ‡	20	504
to Kentucky River	55	559
to the Falls of the Ohio	50	609
to the Wabash, or Ouabache	131	740
to Cherokee River	60	800
to the Missisippi	40	840

N. B. THE places mentioned in the three first Routs are delineated in the foregoing map, by an officer who has an actual knowledge of most of them, and has long served against the Indians. The Fourth Rout down the Ohio was given by an Indian trader, who has often passed from Fort-Pitt to the Falls; and the distances he gives of the mouths of the several rivers that fall into the Ohio may be pretty certainly depended on. Our maps hitherto published are very erroneous in placing some of those rivers.

† These rivers, called Little and Great Mineamie or Miammee, fall into the Ohio between Sioto and the Ouabache, and are different from the Miamis river, which runs into the west end of Lake Erie, below the Miamis fort.

‡ So called from Elephant's bones said to be found there.

APPENDIX

APPENDIX V.

NAMES of different INDIAN NATIONS in NORTH-AMERICA, with the Numbers of their Fighting Men; referred to in the Note, page 94.

THE following lift was drawn up by a French trader, a perfon of confiderable note, who has refided many years among the Indians, and ftill continues at Detroit, having taken the oaths of allegiance to the King of Great Britain. His account may be depended on, fo far as matters of this kind can be brought near the truth; a great part of it being delivered from his own perfonal knowlege.

                                                Warriors

Conawaghrunas, near the falls of St. Louis - - 200
Abenaquis, ⎫ 350
Michmacs, ⎪ 700
* Amaliftes, ⎬ St. Lawrence Indians 550
* Chalas, ⎭ 130
Nipiffins, ⎱ living towards the heads of the 400
Algonquins, ⎰ Ottawa river 300
Les Tetes de Boule, or Round Heads, near the above 2500
Six Nations, on the frontiers of New-York, &c. - 1550
Wiandots, near lake Erie - - - - - - - - 300
Chipwas, ⎱ near the Lakes Superior and Michigan 5000
Ottawas, ⎰ 900

                                       Meffefagues,

Appendix V.

	Warriors
Meſſeſagues, or River Indians, being wandering tribes, on the lakes Huron and Superior, - - - -	2000
Powtewatamis, near St. Joſeph's and Detroit - -	350
Les Puans, } near Puans bay	700
Folle avoine, or Wild-Oat Indians	350
* Mechecouakis, }	250
Sakis, } South of Puans bay	400
Maſcoutens, }	500
Ouiſconſins, on a river of that name, falling into the Miſſiſippi on the eaſt-ſide - - - - - - -	550
Chriſtinaux, } far north, near the lakes	3000
Aſſinaboes, or Aſſinipouals } of the ſame name	1500
Blancs † Barbus, or White Indians with Beards -	1500
Sioux, of the meadows } towards the heads of	2500
Sioux, of the woods } Miſſiſippi	1800
Miſſouri, on the river of that name - - - - -	3000
* Grandes Eaux - - - - - - - - - -	1000
Oſages, }	600
Canſes, }	1600
Panis blancs, } ſouth of Miſſouri	2000
Panis piques, }	1700
Padoucas, }	500
Ajoues, north of the ſame - - - - - - -	1100
Arkanſes, on the river that bears their name, falling into Miſſiſippi on the weſt ſide - - - - -	2000
Alibamous, a tribe of the Creeks - - - - -	600
* Ouanakina }	300
* Chiakaneſſou } Unknown, unleſs the author has put	350
* Machecous } them for tribes of the Creeks	800
* Caouitas }	700
* Souikilas }	200
Miamis, upon the river of that name, falling into Lake Erie, - - - - - - -	350

† They live to the northweſt, and the French, when they firſt ſaw them, took them for Spaniards.

Delawares

Appendix V.

	Warriors
Delawares (les Loups) on the Ohio	600
Shawanefe on Sioto	500
Kickapoos ⎫	300
Ouachtanons ⎬ on the Ouabache	400
Peanquichas ⎭	250
Kafkafquias, or Illinois in general, on the Illinois river	600
* Pianria	800
Catawbas, on the frontiers of North-Carolina	150
Cherokees, behind South-Carolina	2500
Chickafaws ⎫	750
Natchez ⎬ Mobile and Miffifippi	150
Chactaws ⎭	4500
	56,500

THE above lift confifts chiefly of fuch Indians as the French were connected with in Canada and Louifiana. Wherever we knew the names by which the different nations are diftinguifhed by the Englifh, we have inferted them. But the orthography is yet very unfettled, and the feveral nations marked with an * afterifm are unknown to us, and therefore they are left as they ftand in the original lift.

So large a number of fighting men may ftartle us at firft fight; but the account feems no where exaggerated, excepting only that the Catawba nation is now almoft extinct. In fome nations which

which we are acquainted with, the account falls even ſhort of their numbers; and ſome others do not appear to be mentioned at all, or at leaſt not by any name known to us.

SUCH, for inſtance, are the Lower Creeks, of whom we have a liſt according to their towns. In this liſt their warriors or gunſmen are 1180, and their inhabitants about 6000. Thus a comparative judgment may be formed of the nations above-mentioned; the number of whoſe inhabitants will (in this proportion to their warriors, viz. 5 to 1) be about 283,000

THE END.

INDEX.

Amherſt, Genl., Commander-in-Chief, 9.
Arms ſuitable for Indian warfare, 113.
Artificers, organization of, 117.
Attack, mode of general, 134.

Beaver, chief of the Turky Tribe of Delawares, 53, 63.
Benſivaſica, a Shawaneſe chief, 70; ſpeech, 74.
Big Beaver Creek, Bouquet croſſes, 46.
Bouquet, Henry. Biographical Sketch. Charaƈter, xvii; enters the service of the King of Sardinia; battle of Cony, xviii.; ſerves the Prince of Orange; accompanies Lord Middleton to Italy; ſtudies military art, xix; appointed to command in Royal American Corps, xxi; arrives in America, xxii; his death at Penſacola, xxiii; ſent to the relief of Fort Pitt, 10; arrives at Carliſle, 10; at Fort Bedford, 15; at Fort Ligonier, 16; Battle of Buſhy Run, 16-25; arrives at Fort Pitt, 25; Moncrief's "Orders," 27; Expedition againſt the Ohio Indians, 1-81 (ſee under *Expedition*); return to Fort Pitt; to Philadelphia, 81; addreſs of the Pennſylvania General Aſſembly, 82; Bouquet's anſwer, 84; reſolves of Houſe of Burgeſſes of Virginia, Bouquet's reply, 86; promoted, 87.
Bradſtreet's Expedition, xv, 31; treaty with Indians, 36; diſapproved by Genl. Gage, 36; deſpatches to Bouquet, 62.
Buſhy Run, Battle of, 16-25.

Carliſle,

158 Index.

Carlifle, Penn., Bouquet arrives at, 10.
Cafquair's Village and Tribe, 147.
Cherokee River, 143.
Clayton, Lieut. Col. Pennfylvania troops, 87.
Clothing fuitable for foldiers, 111.
Croghan, George, deputy of Sir W. Johnfon, treats with the Shawanefe, 89.
Cumberland, Duke of, xx.
Cuſtaloga, chief of the Wolfe-tribe of Delawares, 53, 63.

Dalyell, Capt., sent to relieve Detroit, 9.
Daurby, Mrs. 144.
Defiles compaffed, 130.
Difpofition to receive the enemy, 131.
Detroit befieged, 8.
Diftances from Fort Pitt to Cuyahoga, 149.
" " " " Junqueindundeh, 150.
" " " " Miamis Fort, 150.
" " " " Miffifippi, 151.
" " Philadelphia to Fort Pitt, 148.
" " Venango to Juniatta, 145.
Dogs, ufe of, in Indian warfare, 116.
Duffaux, Col. Jofeph, of Royal Americans, xx.

Ecuyer, Capt., commands at Fort Pitt, 9.
Encampment, plan of an, 127.
Eweecunwee, a Shawanefe chief, 70.
Exercifes of foldiers, 114.
Expedition againſt the Ohio Indians 1–81 ; Bouquet arrives at Fort Loudoun, 34; at Fort Pitt, 35; fends meffage to the Indians, 37; prepares to march into Ohio, 39; addrefs to troops, 40; order of march, 41 ; leaves Fort Pitt, 44; at Loggftown,

Index.

Loggstown, 45; crosses Big Beaver Creek, 46; crosses Little Beaver Creek, 47; at Yellow Creek, 48; at Nemenshehelas Creek, 49; at Muskingum River, 50; couriers to Bradstreet obliged to return, 50; treats with the Indians, 52; speech to them, 53; delivery of prisoners, 58; resumes march, crosses Margaret Creek, 59; encamps at forks of Muskingum and fortifies, 60; messengers from the Indians, 61; despatches from Col. Bradstreet, 62; treats with the Senecas and Delawares, Kiyashutas' speech, 66, Bouquet's answer, 67; treats with Turky and Turtle Tribes, 68; deposes Nettowhatways, 69; treats with Shawanese; Red Hawke's speech, 70; Bouquet's answer, 72; Benevissico's speech, and the answer, 74; arrival of prisoners in camp, 76; return to Fort Pitt, 81.

Fort Assumption, 143.

Fort Bedford reinforced, 14; Bouquet arrives at, 15.

Fort Chartres, 146.

Fort Ligonier attacked, 13; reinforced, 14; Bouquet arrives at, 16.

Fort Loudoun, Bouquet arrives at, 34.

Fort Pitt besieged, 8.

Forts, construction of, against Indians, 137.

Forty-second regiment, 10, 32.

Fox, Joseph, Speaker of Pennsylvania General Assembly, 83.

Francis, Lieut. Col. of Pennsylvania troops, 87.

French cession of Canada, etc., 3.

French Forts in Louisiana ceded, 141.

Frontiers over-run by the Indians, 6.

Gage, Genl., Commander-in-Chief, 31; refuses to ratify Bradstreet's treaty, 36.

Gladwin, Major, at Detroit, xiv, 8.

Great Mineamie or Miammee River, 152.

Hutchins,

Hutchins, Thomas, xv.
Illinois River, 143.
Indian character, xii; temper and genius, 95.
Indian nations, names of, and number of warriors, 153.
Indian towns on or near the Ohio River, 149.
Indian tribes—
  Cafquairs, 147.
  Caughnawagas, 63, 75.
  Chipwas, 31, 56.
  Delawares, 5, 31, 36, 39, 45, 46, 51, 58, 62, 65, 66, 68, 73, 75, 89, 142.
  Kafkafquais, 146.
  Metches, 146.
  Mingoes, 31, 46.
  Mohickons, 31.
  Ottawas, 31, 56, 63.
  Pianquichas, 144.
  Senecas, 52, 66, 73, 75, 89, 142.
  Shawanefe, 5, 31, 36, 39, 45, 46, 51, 58, 62, 64, 65, 68, 70, 75, 88, 142.
  Six Nations, 38, 56.
  Wiandots, 31, 56, 64, 142.
Jeffereys, Col. C., of the Royal Americans, xx.
John, Capt. (Indian), prifoner at Fort Pitt, 68.
Johnfon, Sir William, empowered to make peace with the Indians, 67, 91.

Kafkafquias River and Tribe, 145.
Keigleighque, a Shawanefe chief, 70.
Keiffinautchtha, a Shawanefe chief, 53, 70.
Kelappama, brother of the Turtle chief, 68.
Kiyafhuta, chief of the Senecas 52; fpeech, 66.

La Bay,

Index.

La Bay, Fort, captured, 6.
La Prairie du Rocher, 146.
Laviffimo, a Shawanefe chief, 70.
Lawaughqua, a Shawanefe chief, fpeech, 89.
Le Boeuf, Fort, captured, 6.
Light troops for fervice in the woods, 111, 116.
Line of march in Indian warfare, 128.
Little Beaver Creek, 47.
Little Mineamie or Miammee River, 152.
Loggftown, Bouquet arrives at, 46.

Miamis, Fort, captured, 6.
Miamis River, 152.
Michilimackinac, Fort, captured, 6.
Miffifippi River, 152.
Moncrief, Major, "orders" to Col. Bouquet, 27.
Mufkingum, Indians retreat to, 30; Bouquet arrives at, 50.

Negroes in Illinois, 147.
Nettowhatways, chief of the Turtle tribe of Delawares, depofed, 69.
Nimwha, a Shawanefe chief, 70.

Ohio Indians, expedition againft, 1–81.
Ouabache River, 143.
Ouachtanon, Fort, captured, 6.
Ourry, Capt., commands at Fort Bedford, 14.

Parkman, Francis, prefatory remarks, xi.
Peace of 1763, xi; effect on the Indians, xii.
Penn, Governor, addrefs to the volunteers, 33.
Pennfylvania General Affembly, addrefs to Bouquet, 82.
Peter, chief of Caughnawagas, 62.

Pipe,

Pipe, Capt. (Indian), prifoner at Fort Pitt, 48.
Pontiac's confpiracy, xiii.
Preparations neceffary for Indian warfare, 123.
Prefqu' Ifle, Fort, captured, 6.
Prevoft, Lt. Col. Aug., 60th Regt., xxiii.
Prevoft, Col. James, of Royal Americans, xx.
Prifoners, arrival at camp, affecting fcenes, 75.
Prifoners delivered to Bouquet, 58, 63, 64, 72.

Red Hawke, a Shawanefe chief, fpeech, 70.
Reflections on the war with the favages, 93.
Reid, Col., fecond in command, 87.
Rock Meadow, 146.
Roman method of warfare adapted to Indian warfare, 102.
Royal American corps organized, xx.

St. Jofephs, Fort, captured, 6.
Sandufky, Fort, captured, 6.
Settlements, method of forming, on the frontiers, 119; plan of, 121.
Seventy-feventh regiment, 10.
Sixtieth regiment, 32.
Smallman, Mr., delivered up by the Indians, 64.
Smith, William, author of this work, xv.
Square, to reduce the, 132.
Stanwix, Col. J., of Royal Americans, xx.

Venango, Fort, captured, 6.
Vincennes, Fort, 143.
Virginia Houfe of Burgeffes, refolves to Bouquet, 86.

Wabafh River, 143.

Yellow Creek, Bouquet at, 48.
Yorke, Sir Joseph, xxi.

www.ingramcontent.com/pod-product-compliance
Lightning Source LLC
Chambersburg PA
CBHW030819190426
43197CB00036B/606